Seven Keys to Financial Freedom

Steven & Christine,

May God Bless you
with financial freedom
and use you to lead
many others to
freedom in Christ!

Jim

7 Keys to Financial Freedom

By Jon Byler
Copywrite © 2005 by Jon Byler
ISBN-13: 978-0-9770085-0-6
ISBN-10: 0-9770085-0-9

7 Keys to Financial Freedom

Unlock the door to God's blessing in your finances

Rev. Jon Byler

LeadersServe

Dedicated to my father, Raymond Byler, who more than anyone else I know modeled these principles and taught me financial freedom. I believe that he is now enjoying the treasure he sent ahead while he was on this earth.

CONTENTS

Key Verses:

"Whoever can be trusted with very little can also be trusted with much, and whoever is dishonest with very little will also be dishonest with much. So if you have not been trustworthy in handling worldly wealth, who will trust you with true riches?"
(Lk. 16:10-11)

FOREWORD

Too often, sermons and teaching on finances center around giving people 'tricks' on how to prosper and make enough money. We often hear a preacher tell the audience, "Give so much and God will give you three times in return for what you have given". Such a poor handling of this important topic has contributed to the "casino" mentality among many Christians who behave as if God operates a lottery company and all you need to do is give so much and wait for an instant miracle!

Many times the approach taken is either too simplistic or so narrow that those who apply the tricks end up being frustrated because they don't work. The reason for this is that the subject of money is a broad one and can't be mastered by simply applying one scriptural principle. Neither does true prosperity come from having a certain preacher lay hands on you, but rather by learning and practicing the time tested biblical principles as Jon teaches in this book, *The Seven Keys To Financial Freedom*.

It has been a great pleasure and privilege for me to know and work with Rev. Jon Byler since 1991, when he came to Kenya to work with our church as a missionary. He served as the pastor of one of our churches at Juja for over five years. In 1996 Rev. Byler moved on to serve as the Director of the Centre for Christian Discipleship (CCD), a position he held until January 2003 when he moved from CCD to take up the position of Senior Pastor of Christian Church International, Thika.

The principles Jon teaches in this book of "Seven Keys to Financial Freedom" have been tested in a number of our Churches and the impact has been remarkable. In 1994 Jon taught the same principles outlined in this book at one of our branch Churches in Makueni District. The pastor of that church testified of how the church finances went up after the seminar. In 2001 I invited Jon to teach these principles in our local church. After the teachings we saw a 71% increase in income. I believe that God's principles work! I strongly recommend this book particularly to pastors, church leaders and all those who desire to enjoy financial freedom in their lives, ministries and businesses.

-Henry Z Mulandi, International Director for African Christian Missions International.

INTRODUCTION

Money, money, money. Someone has said that you can't live with it and you can't live without it! All of us use money. We work for money; we use money to buy food and to pay for our housing. We exchange money for clothes or education. Our lives touch money nearly every day and the money touches us! It is an area of our lives that is universally painful to discuss and change. Finances are also one of the major areas of conflict in marriages and homes.

There are many conflicting views concerning this issue of money, some of which are culturally based and some of which are simply personal opinions.

I am thankful that the Bible offers a lot of advice on this issue. Most believers are surprised that the Bible has so much to say concerning our money, how we earn it, how we spend it, how we give it and many other things. The book of Proverbs is full of verses about money. I read Proverbs and found over 125 verses directly related to money, our attitude towards money, the causes of poverty, the blessings of God, etc. Jesus spoke more about finances than perhaps any other single subject. Yet someone has noted that the last part of a man to be saved is his pocket! Is your pocket saved?

The Christian church has received much teaching about tithing and I certainly believe in tithing. But God's concern for our finances goes much deeper than whether or not we are tithing. There are many other key principles in scripture that relate to our finances that also need to be obeyed if we are to experience God's fullest blessing. And my wish for you is that as you put God's principles concerning finances into practice in your life you will experience his fullest blessing. It has been my joy to teach this material to hundreds of people whose lives have been positively changed as a result. As you read, look for the keys that will unlock the doors of his blessings in your life. The study guide included in this edition is intended for group or personal study. A leaders' guide is available upon request from the author.

I acknowledge the blessing that many people have been to my life through books and through their teaching. Very few of the ideas presented in this book originated with me. See the bibliography for some of the books that have shaped my life. I also want to thank my wonderful wife, Loice, for her constant support and encouragement in my life as a husband and as a writer. Thanks also to Paul and Bertha Swarr for their assistance in proofreading the manuscript.

May God bless you and give you financial freedom!

Jon Byler
4th printing June 2005

KEY ONE

Recognize Finances as a Spiritual Issue

"No one can serve two masters. Either he will hate the one and love the other, or he will be devoted to the one and despise the other. You cannot serve both God and money." (Mt. 6:24)

KEY ONE: RECOGNIZE FINANCES AS A SPIRITUAL ISSUE

If we view money as only a material thing without any spiritual power in our lives we make a grave mistake. As I have looked at this issue and reflected on what scripture says about money (and it says a lot), I am convinced that we need to recognize our finances are a spiritual issue. Why do I believe this?

Finances have the ability to become God in our lives.
The first reason that I view finances as a spiritual issue is that the Bible makes it clear that money has the power to become a rival god in my life. The Bible refers to *"unrighteous mammon"* Mt. 6:24, *"No one can serve two masters. Either he will hate the one and love the other, or he will be devoted to the one and despise the other. You cannot serve both God and money"* ("unrighteous mammon," KJV). Money has the potential to be our master, in fact it will compete with our allegiance to God. When we find that our hearts are being drawn by money or our decisions are being based on money and profit only or when we find that more and more of our time is involved in the pursuit of making money, it is time for a spiritual checkup. Finances, more than any other area of our lives, have the ability to draw us slowly and

subtly away from God. Finances are tricky and often affect us without our conscious knowledge. Maybe this is why Jesus talked about the "deceitfulness of riches." (Mt. 13:22)

Mt. 6:31-33 also confirms that it is possible to seek after material things more than the kingdom of God. *"So do not worry, saying, 'What shall we eat?' or 'What shall we drink?' or 'What shall we wear?' For the pagans run after all these things, and your heavenly Father knows that you need them. But seek first his kingdom and his righteousness, and all these things will be given to you as well."*

I was talking with one of my neighbors one day and as we talked he startled me when he boldly stated, "My god is money." While I weep for his spiritual condition, I think he should be commended for his honesty! Most people who worship money don't have the insight or courage to admit the reality of what their lives reflect.

Finances can be used of God to direct our lives.

The second reason that I believe that our finances are a spiritual issue is that our finances can be used of God to direct our lives. As with other things in our lives, God can speak to us through finances. Whether finances are in short supply or in abundance, often God makes known to us his will for our lives through finances. We need to recognize this and submit to it. If there is no money for a house, perhaps God doesn't want us to build right then; if there is no money to expand the business, perhaps God is saying that we should wait. **God can indicate his timing for us in his provision or withholding of finances.** We must be broken to his will in order to hear him clearly. So many times in our finances God wants to deal with us but we are blind to what he is saying.

We might run out and borrow the money, or we take another job to earn the money, or we make foolish decisions because we failed to hear God speaking to our situation. In Acts 18:1-5 it appears that Paul did tent making until God provided support for him to preach full time.

When my wife and I felt that God had called us to Kenya from the USA, we made preparations. But in the area of finances we had to wait on God. We told God, "When you are ready for us to go, provide the remaining amount of money." It would have been easy to try to "help" God by borrowing or using other means to raise money, but his will was for us to wait. I am now waiting on money to buy another car. When God provides, I will rejoice. Until then, I ask him to keep the old one running!

When we face financial difficulties, we need to remember James 1:2-3, *"Consider it pure joy, my brothers, whenever you face trials of many kinds, because you know that the testing of your faith develops perseverance,"* and Rom. 8:28, *"And we know that in all things God works for the good of those who love him, who have been called according to his purpose."*

God uses the trials of money to teach us many things. We must acknowledge that and begin to look for those things.

There can be many reasons that God does not provide finances for us at a particular point in our lives. Following are several of them:

1. We don't need it.

God may not provide because what we think is a "need" is a "want." We can do without it.

2. To test our faith.

Sometimes God waits to provide in order to strengthen our faith. If everything came to us easily and quickly, how would our faith increase?

3. We have misspent.

At other times we don't receive because we have not wisely used what God has given to us. This is a rebuke or reproof that is designed to teach us an important lesson.

4. We may have violated Scriptural principles in finances.

We can't expect God's blessing when we are violating what we know as his will. We need to check ourselves and study God's word to know the will of God.

5. God wants a major change in method, direction or location.

God can withhold finances to help us realize that he wants us to go in another direction. When we are headed in the right way the finances will be provided.

In a situation where we experience lack of finances we should pray to know which one(s) of the above reasons apply to our particular situation.

Faithfulness in finances can be a stepping-stone to more responsibility.

Another principle in scripture concerning our finances is that how we use our money is an indicator of spiritual maturity and can be a stepping-stone to more responsibility.

Lk. 16:10-11, *"Whoever can be trusted with very little can also be trusted with much, and whoever is dishonest with very little will also be dishonest with much. So if you have not been trustworthy in handling worldly wealth, who will trust you with true riches?"* This verse is saying that before we can be entrusted with "true riches," we must correctly handle worldly riches, i.e. money. God cannot fully bless your spiritual ministry if your finances are in disarray. This does not mean that he cannot use you, but he cannot fully bless you until you are correctly handling your finances. This principle applies in our personal lives as well as in ministries and churches. This is a principle that must be taken seriously by persons from all cultures and all nations.

Another verse directed to leaders demonstrates the same principle, *"He must manage his own family well and see that his children obey him with proper respect. If anyone does not know how to manage his own family, how can he take care of God's church?"* (1 Tim. 3:4-5) Again there is a progression. First, manage your family, including finances, and then you will be able to work in the church.

Recognize that finances really are a spiritual issue. The way you handle money says more about the condition of your heart than your testimony. Try to win your landlord to Christ when you are behind on your rent or witness to the person at the corner shop where you owe money!

Action Point: Take a few moments to examine your life. Have you recognized the power of money in your life? What are some of the ways that God has used money to direct you and what did you learn from it?

KEY TWO

LEARN CONTENTMENT

"I have learned to be content…" (Phil. 4:11-12)

KEY TWO:
LEARN THE SECRET OF
CONTENTMENT

Alice and James were a typical couple. They worked hard at their jobs and had great dreams for their future. However, in spite of their best efforts, they never seemed to have enough. Jim tried working longer hours and for a time that seemed to help. With the extra income they were able to enroll their children in a better school and buy a new colour TV. Still, many of their dreams were out of reach and the daily strain began to take its toll on their relationship. Every time money was mentioned, an argument followed. James was always tired physically and didn't have the time or energy to strengthen relationships with Alice or the children. He felt trapped in a never-ending cycle of working harder to pay overdue bills. He longed for relief and prayed that he would get a promotion that would solve their financial problems. "If only we could get more," he thought, "we would be happy." Alice was frustrated that she couldn't afford the new fashions that she longed to wear and was embarrassed when friends visited and found that her sofa had torn fabric on it. She thought to herself, "If only I could get a new sofa set and a few dresses, I would be happy."

James and Alice were missing something that many people never find: contentment. Contentment is a rare virtue in our society. Our modern world is filled with advertising designed to create in us a desire to have the product that is being offered. We are daily bombarded with reminders of what we don't have and what we should have in order to be happy. Ironically, a biblical key to financial freedom is to learn the secret of contentment. Contentment simply means being satisfied with what I have. In this light, God's instructions about contentment need careful observation.

THE CALL TO CONTENTMENT

Paul makes a powerful statement when he says, *"... I have learned to be content whatever the circumstances. I know what it is to be in need, and I know what it is to have plenty. I have learned the secret of being content in any and every situation, whether well fed or hungry, whether living in plenty or in want."* (Phil. 4:11-12) His words call us today to examine our attitude towards our possessions and to learn his secret of contentment. He teaches us two things about contentment.

Contentment can be learned

Notice that Paul says that he "learned" to be content. He was not born content; it was something that he had to learn. He learned it through experience. He had experience with little and he had experience with plenty. He probably made some mistakes and some days found himself wallowing in self pity because his sandals were not as nice as Lydia's! If only he could have that purple robe instead of his brown one; he could preach with more anointing! Oops, he realized that he needed to get his mind straight and back in line with the word of God. Learning always takes effort and Paul had to make the effort required to learn. It will not be easy for you to learn contentment but it can be done.

Contentment is not based on possessions.

Paul indicates that he has learned to be content with little and with much. That's not an easy task. Most of us, like James and Alice, fall into the trap of thinking, "If only I had a little more, I would be happy."

But it's not true. Possessions will never bring happiness. A millionaire was asked one time, "How much is enough?" He replied, "A little more." Although he had all that his heart could desire, he was not contented. He was still looking for something else.

The human heart is deceitful. If we have only a radio we think, "If only I could have a TV, I would be so happy." After some time we are able to buy an old black and white TV and we are ecstatic! Watching the news was never so good. But as time goes by we begin to think, "You know, black and white is okay, but it would surely be nice to have a colour set." After we have a colour set we really need "one with a remote control". The story never ends! The world is filled with people looking for the one more "thing" that will bring them happiness. It may be a new suit or dress, the latest hairstyle or computer, a better car, their own house, a better job, a new sofa set, or an opportunity to travel. But Paul teaches us that contentment is not based on how much we have. He learned that it is possible to be content with little and also possible to be content with much.

This lesson is no less difficult for rich people to learn than poor people because it is not an external issue; it is a heart issue. Take a look at your heart. Are you content with what you have or are there constant thoughts in your mind that you must get more? I think I'm most tempted in the area of electronics, especially computers. I remember a time that I was consumed with the desire to get a newer, faster computer. I saw them advertised in every newspaper and in every shop they seemed to scream for my attention. At last I had to ask myself, "What is my current computer not able to do?" I had to admit that there was nothing that it could not do, I had just fallen for the advertising gimmicks that bigger and faster is better.

What was Paul's "secret"? How did he learn this difficult lesson? I believe that the reason that Paul was able to be content was that he learned to focus on God instead of material things. He says in the next verse, "I can do everything through him who gives me strength." That focus enabled Paul to keep going even when there was lack. It also enabled him to keep his perspective when he had more than enough.

The Bible also gives us many other instructions concerning the issue of contentment. Consider the following verses:

Prov. 30:8, *"Keep falsehood and lies far from me; give me neither poverty nor riches, but give me only my daily bread."*

Heb. 13:5, *"Keep your lives free from the love of money and be content with what you have, because God has said, 'Never will I leave you; never will I forsake you.'"* Our security is in God's presence; not in what we have.

Lk. 12:15, *"Watch out! Be on your guard against all kinds of greed; a man's life does not consist in the abundance of his possessions."* (See also Ps. 49:16-20)

> **We must deal with our motive for desiring material gain.**

We normally measure a person by how much he has, and we think that the more we get the better we will be. However, the Bible exposes this as false.

1 Tim. 6:6, *"But godliness with contentment is great gain."* It is of great benefit to have salvation and to be content with what we have. Some have godliness without contentment, and possibly others have contentment without godliness. Put them together and you have a powerful combination.

Ecc. 5:10, *"Whoever loves money never has money enough; whoever loves wealth is never satisfied with his income."*

Are you content? Or do you find yourself constantly looking around at others, desiring to have what they have? God desires for each of us to experience contentment.

THE ENEMIES OF CONTENTMENT

There are several things that keep us from being content...

Placing our security in possessions.

Money can quickly become our security in life, and in that way it has become our God. Jesus clearly says, *"You cannot serve both God and money."* (Mt. 6:24) God or money will occupy the supreme place in our lives. God's desire is that we find our sense of security in him alone.

However, our human tendency is to feel secure only when we feel that we have enough money or material possessions. If the bank account is empty we feel uncertain about the future. If we don't have enough for the rent at the end of the month, we begin to worry. These are signals that we are placing our security in money rather than God.

Our contentment cannot come from money; it must come from God. When we try to find security in material things, we will always be disappointed. Countless persons throughout history have tried it and discovered in the end that money doesn't satisfy the deepest needs in the heart. That's why Solomon could say, *"Whoever loves wealth is never satisfied with his income..."* (Ecc. 5:10) He also said, *"Whoever trusts in his riches will fall, but the righteous will thrive like a green leaf."* (Prov. 11:28) How can you know if your security is based on your possessions? Ask yourself, "What would happen to me today if I lost everything I owned? How would I respond?"

Desiring to get rich.

A second enemy of contentment is a desire to get rich. If I went to the street and stopped 100 people who were passing and asked, "Do you want to be rich?" I imagine that at least 99 of them would say emphatically, "Yes!" We dream of having all the money we want and it seems that most of our problems would be solved if only we could have a little more money. Secretly, and in some cases openly, many of us desire to get rich!

A desire to get rich may seem like a godly thing but according to the scripture it is not so. Consider what the following verses say about desiring to get rich...

Prov 23:4, *"Do not wear yourself out to get rich; have the wisdom to show restraint."*

Prov 28:20, *"A faithful man will be richly blessed, but one eager to get rich will not go unpunished."*

Prov 28:22, *"A stingy man is eager to get rich and is unaware that poverty awaits him."*

1 Tim. 6:9-10, *"People who want to get rich fall into temptation and a trap and into many foolish and harmful desires that plunge men into ruin and destruction. For the love of money is a root of all kinds of evil. Some* *people, eager for money, have wandered from the faith and pierced themselves with many griefs."* (See also vs. 6-8)

Notice that these verses do not say that it is a sin to be rich; instead they look at our heart's desire. When the desire to become rich is ruling our lives we cannot prosper and, according to Paul, we may even lose our salvation. We must deal with our motive for desiring material gain. Do we want to get rich just to have an easy life? That is a selfish motive. On the other hand, if we genuinely desire to expand the kingdom of God with our wealth, that is a different motive altogether. 2 Cor. 9:11 gives God's reason for making us rich, *"...So that you can be generous on every occasion..."* God wants to give blessings to those that will channel the blessings to others.

While it is not a sin to be rich, the scriptures clearly warn of the dangers that riches bring to our lives. See **Mt. 13:22**; and **19:23-26** for two examples in addition to the ones mentioned. Riches are not the solution to our problems as much as we would like to think!

Does this mean that we can't try to improve our lives? Certainly not! We should work hard and do our best to see God's blessing in our finances and possessions. There is nothing wrong with that, as we will see later in this study. We should experience all the blessings that God has for us. But we must guard our hearts against ungodly desires. The desire to get rich will keep us from being contented.

We should recognize that our society glorifies wealth and possessions. Success is viewed in terms of how much we have. The media constantly reminds us that we don't have enough. It generally portrays those who have a lot of money as happy and satisfied in life and slowly leads us to think that wealth is the answer to our problems. We need to meditate on what God's word says about riches.

Valuing riches more than character.

A third enemy of contentment is to value riches more than character. The world usually judges people by how much they have materially. Character flaws in wealthy persons are easily overlooked. However, God judges us, not by our wealth, but by our character. *"The LORD does not look at the things man looks at. Man looks at the outward appearance, but the LORD looks at the heart."* (1 Sam. 16:7)

How do you judge yourself? How do you judge others? What do you pray for when you pray for yourself? Is it material things or development of character? When you start thinking more about what you have than who you are, you are valuing riches more than character. As I looked at the book of Proverbs I was astonished to find out how much it had to say about this issue. Consider the following verses:

Prov 3:13-16, *"Blessed is the man who finds wisdom, the man who gains understanding, for she is more profitable than silver and yields better returns than gold. She is more precious than rubies; nothing you desire can compare with her. Long life is in her right hand; in her left hand are riches and honor. A kindhearted woman gains respect, but ruthless men gain only wealth."* (Underlining mine)

Prov 17:16, *"Of what use is money in the hand of a fool, since he has no desire to get wisdom?"*

Prov 19:1, *"Better a poor man whose walk is blameless than a fool whose lips are perverse."*

Prov 19:22, *"What a man desires is unfailing love; better to be poor than a liar."*

Prov 22:1, *"A good name is more desirable than great riches; to be esteemed is better than silver or gold."*

Prov 28:11, *"A rich man may be wise in his own eyes, but a poor man who has discernment sees through him."*

In summary, Proverbs teaches that wisdom is better than riches; a clean life is better than riches; it is better to be poor than to be a liar; a good name is better than riches; and it is better to have discernment than to have riches. These verses are not teaching that wealth is wrong but they warn us against the tendency of the human heart to value the external over the internal. It is all too easy to judge someone based on his economic status rather than the strength of his character.

Our key verses (Lk. 17:10-11) make it clear that material wealth is not "true" riches. We should not base our life on secondary riches but seek for the riches of heaven.

Guard your heart against these three enemies of contentment. Take time to pray about them and allow God to deal with your heart condition. Then follow the path to contentment.

THE PATH TO CONTENTMENT

Contentment looks so elusive and slippery. Is it really possible for one to be content in today's society? How can we learn contentment? Let's look at three steps to contentment.

Recognize that God is the owner of everything.

Before we can fully begin to experience contentment and unlock the door to God's blessings in our finances, we need to recognize that he is the true owner of everything that we possess. We tend to think in terms of "my account, my vehicle, my house" but the Bible gives a much *different picture. Look at what God says…*

"The silver is mine and the gold is mine, declares the LORD Almighty." (Hag. 2:8) This means that God owns the cash in your pocket and all bank and savings accounts!

Let's go a step further. In Ps. 50:10 God says, *"For every animal of the forest is mine, and the cattle on a thousand hills."* Do you own any animals? Cows, chickens, or goats? They belong to God! In the agricultural society of the Old Testament, animals were often the primary asset that a person possessed. Today God might say to us, "Your business, your car, your clothes, furniture, TV, and kitchen utensils are all mine!"

"Okay", you might say, "God owns everything, but at least I have a title deed for my land!" Sorry, but God says, *"The land must not be sold permanently, because the land is mine and you are but aliens and my tenants."* (Leviticus 25:23) God even owns "our" land! His title deed is stronger than ours!

If God owns everything that I possess, what am I doing with all these things? Our second step answers this question.

Realize that you are a steward.

While God owns everything that you have, he entrusts possessions to you for a time. The Bible teaches that your role is that of a steward or manager. (See Lk. 12:42-48 and Mt. 25:14-30). A steward is someone who takes care of the owner's possessions on behalf of the owner. The steward always handles the possessions with the goal of doing whatever the owner desires to be done. He asks himself, "What does the owner want? How would he use this resource?"

This attitude has profound implications for the believer. When you begin to see the things that you have as God's, but entrusted to you for a time, you will begin to approach life from a totally different perspective. Yes, the house you "own" is for you to use, but if the true owner says, "I'm sending a visitor over who needs a room for the night," you are supposed to say, "Yes, sir!" You can use the money in "your" bank account but when God says, "Give a day's wages to that needy person," you should respond with action!

The realization that you are a steward of God's possessions is a big step towards contentment. It shifts your goal from getting rich to desiring to glorify God with what you have. Instead of finding your security in the things that you have, you are able to trust the owner to supply all your needs. You will desire to be more faithful as a manager so that the owner will entrust more to you. You will begin to value the things that the owner values.

Release your possessions to God.

The final step to contentment is to yield your possessions to God. When you realize that God owns everything and has entrusted things to you it is extremely helpful to consciously acknowledge God's ownership by giving back to him what belongs to him.

As I have taught this concept in many churches, I have found that many people have been helped to release "their things" to God by listing all the significant items they possess and then signing it over to God. Try it! Review the scriptures we have looked at and then use the "Deed Of Transfer" on the next page to give God his rightful place in your finances. List all items that are valuable to you: bank accounts, cash, land, vehicles, clothes, TV, etc. When you finish, have someone sign as a witness to what you have done. If you are married, do this together as a couple. Then take some time in prayer, asking God to help you be faithful as a steward of whatever you have now and whatever you will receive in the future. Congratulations! You have taken a giant step towards living a contented life and unlocking God's blessings on your finances.

DEED OF TRANSFER

I, _____, (your name) understand that God is the true owner of all my possessions and that he has called me to be a steward. I will experience contentment as I surrender "my" possessions to him.

Therefore, I do release the following possessions into the hand of the Almighty God:

1.

2.

3.

4.

5.

6.

7.

8.

9.

10.

Signed: _____

Date: _____

Witness: _____

KEY THREE

OBEY BIBLICAL
PRINCIPLES OF EARNING

"The blessing of the Lord brings wealth, and he adds no trouble to it." (Prov. 10:22)

KEY THREE:
OBEY BIBLICAL PRINCIPLES OF EARNING

James was exhausted. He had just come from the office after a long day of work. On the way home he stopped at the small business that he and his wife had started to make ends meet. He felt as though he had been working night and day for months. Still, the bills seemed to be piling up. He was behind on paying school fees and the rent was also overdue. What could he do? The business was already running 7 days a week and still seemed to be making very little income. He had already tried to reduce expenses by reporting less than his actual income for tax purposes and paying the workers as little as possible. Without money for capital, expansion was nearly impossible. At work he had already had a secret meeting with his friend in management asking for a promotion. But, in spite of the small "gift" he had given his friend, nothing had happened. That night while lying in bed he reflected on his life. Something was wrong. He no longer felt close to his wife and children and seldom had time to say more than a few words to any of them. "If only I could get more money from somewhere…" he thought, as he drifted off to sleep.

We all need and desire money. Money is such a powerful force in our lives that we can easily fall into the trap of desiring to get money more than anything else. It can become a priority in our lives to the extent that we are willing to compromise biblical principles just to get more money. We may do this consciously when we know the commands of God or unconsciously when we are ignorant of what he expects. How we earn our money is important to God. The first two keys dealt with our heart attitudes towards money; this key deals with how we obtain money. The final keys will deal with how we use money.

Prov. 10:22 provides the foundation for this key, *"The blessing of the LORD brings wealth, and he adds no trouble to it."* Wealth can be ablessing and when it comes from the Lord it will not come with "trouble." If the way we are getting money brings trouble with it, something is not right.

Prov 1:19 makes it clear that money obtained in the wrong way is not so good. *"Such is the end of all who go after ill-gotten gain; it takes away the lives of those who get it."* (Italics mine) From these verses it is clear that there are right and wrong ways to obtain money. Let's examine seven principles that the Bible gives about earning money.

Principle One: Work hard

The Bible makes a clear connection between our effort and God'sblessing. Consider Solomon's words, *"All hard work brings a profit, but mere talk leads only to poverty."* (Prov. 14:23) This verse gives us one of the causes of poverty: talking instead of working! Many people are dreaming of the day when God will bless their finances or when someone will give them a big donation. They talk a lot but do little work. They need to wake up and get busy! It sounds very spiritual to "trust God to supply" and this is certainly a biblical principle. But it does not give us permission to sleep all day and then exercise faith! The Bible has much to say about those who sleep instead of work. Consider the following verses...

Prov. 10:4, *"Lazy hands make a man poor, but diligent hands bring wealth."*

Prov. 6:10-11, *"A little sleep, a little slumber, a little folding of the hands to rest— and poverty will come on you like a bandit and scarcity like an armed man."* 2 Thess. 3:6,10,12, *"In the name of the Lord Jesus*

Christ, we command you, brothers, to keep away from every brother who is idle... For even when we were with you we gave you this rule: 'If a man will not work, he shall not eat.'... Such people we command and urge in the Lord Jesus Christ to settle down and earn the bread they eat."

These are strong words! Paul makes it very clear that it is shameful for a brother not to work, to just be idle. Yet many people are in the habit of being idle all day. Every corner is filled with people standing around watching the world go by! When evening comes they decide that it's time to "visit the brethren." Coincidently, their visit comes right at the time for tea and doesn't end until after supper is served! The following night they find another home to visit and life continues! Paul advises that we should keep away from such people and certainly we should not feed them. They need to learn the truth of Prov. 16:26, *"The laborer's appetite works for him; his hunger drives him on."* (Note that this applies to those that will not work; not those who cannot work or who are unable to find work. It is right to give assistance to such people.)

As a pastor, many times young people would come to me and ask for assistance to go on a mission. I usually gave them this reply, "I'd love to help you go on the mission. Why don't you come to my house tomorrow and I'll give you some work to earn the money you need." Some were willing, but many responded, "Oh, I have another commitment tomorrow!" They wanted a free gift but were not willing to work.

If you are not employed, find something to do. How many places have you tried to find a job? It can be very discouraging but don't expect doors to open without a lot of knocking! Even if you need to volunteer your services, you will feel better at the end of the day when you have done something productive. Clean the church compound, dig someone's garden, or wash someone's vehicle. Go to a prospective boss and tell him that you are willing to work for him for one day absolutely free. At the end of the day he can choose whether or not to employ you. He will have gained a day of labour and at least you will have done something productive for the day.

God cannot and will not reward laziness. Laziness brings poverty, not blessing. Many people see work as a curse and assume that work is a part of sin but the Bible teaches that work is honourable. Man was commanded to work before sin came into the world (see Gen. 2:15). Sin brought frustration and sweat to work but did not make it sinful. Therefore, don't look down on work. You were created by God to work! Work is GOOD! God is concerned about how we approach work. Do you see your work as a troublesome necessity? Many people wish that they could stop working and just enjoy life. Why not start enjoying your work? Put your heart into the work you are doing and you'll see an incredible difference in the results. Paul says, *"Serve wholeheartedly, as if you were serving the Lord, not men."* (Eph. 6:7) When you are at work, put your mind there and do your best!

Your work should be top quality, the best that you are able to do, since you are really working for the Lord. If it is sweeping the floor, make it clean enough for a king! If it is woodworking, make sure the joints are well made. If it is keeping accounts, get them to balance perfectly. Put your heart into what you are doing and God will be pleased with it.

I'm afraid that too many believers want *promotion* without *devotion*! They want *inspiration* without *perspiration*; and the *sweets* without the *sweat*! Be willing to work hard. Go the second mile. Be the first to arrive at your working place and the last to leave. Learn to do your job well and then ask God for a promotion. GOD HONOURS HARD WORK!

Principle Two: Don't Work Too Much!

Most people need the challenge of the first principle but some need to hear the second one: Don't work too much! When we learn that "hard work brings profit" it looks attractive to work night and day. That's what happened to James. He needed to hear Solomon's words in Prov. 23:4, *"Do not wear yourself out to get rich; have the wisdom to show restraint."*

When you find that you no longer have any time for your family or time for the things of God, you are working too much. You should not have to wear yourself out trying to make money and get rich; you need to show some restraint. This is especially difficult if you are in business for yourself. When you work in your own business it seems that every hour you work you make more money. So the temptation is to work more and more. Have the wisdom to know when to shut down the business and do something that may be more important.

While some women may struggle with this, I believe it is a special temptation for men. Men feel strongly the responsibility of providing for the family. Of course providing for your family is good and God expects you to provide for them. But realize that your family needs YOU as well as the money that you work to provide. Have the wisdom to show restraint. Know when to quit and do something with your family or for the kingdom of God. Sometimes the family needs you more than your money! Ask yourself, "Am I working too much?"

As a pastor I often prayed with people who were unemployed. Many times we saw God honour our prayers and provide work for the person. Then I often observed that the person had less and less time for the church and for God's work. He would first start missing a fellowship and then he had no time for prayer and finally would even miss the Sunday service. Is this what God intended when he provided a job? I don't think so.

The key here is balance. If we don't work enough we can't expectGod to bless the labour of our hands. But if we work too much we again find that our life is out of balance and God's blessing is withheld. Identify which temptation is the strongest for you and ask God to help you to find the right balance.

Principle Three: Treat others Fairly

In your effort to get money for yourself you can quickly forget your relationships with other people. It is tempting to think that since you need money so much, you can take advantage of others to further your own cause. This may not be done consciously, but often happens without realizing what is being done.

One way that this can be done is by **oppressing the poor**. God has a special place in his heart for the poor and a special place in his judgment for those who oppress the poor. Any time that you take advantage of someone else to profit yourself, this is a sin in God's eyes. Prov 22:16 says, *"He who oppresses the poor to increase his wealth and he who gives gifts to the rich—both come to poverty."* If you hire someone and fail to pay that person a reasonable wage you are oppressing them. We need to look at more than just what others are being paid and ask ourselves, "Can that person live on what I am giving them?"

Don't take advantage of someone just because he/she is not well dressed or educated. In most countries there are certain jobs that are filled by unskilled and often uneducated persons. What position is that in your county? Are these persons fairly paid? It is easy to take advantage of those who are poor or uneducated. James 5:4 speaks about the rich persons who have oppressed others, *"Look! The wages you failed to pay the workmen who mowed your fields are crying out against you."* In our story James thought he would get more profit if he underpaid his workers but it was a form of oppression that God hated.

If you have others working for you, are you dealing with them fairly? Do you give what you promised to them? Do you compensate them for overtime work? Do you speak to them as though they are human beings with thoughts and feelings? I recall a time that I was purchasing an item in a store and the sales attendant was trying to demonstrate how the item worked but was unable to get it plugged in. The boss came around and saw his struggling and asked, "Don't you have any brains?" I wanted to ask the boss, "Do you normally choose employees who don't have brains?" That was verbal oppression. The humorous conclusion is that the boss grabbed the item and with an air of superiority, tried to plug it in. He couldn't do it either! I tried not to laugh out loud as I wondered, "What happened to *your* brains?"

If you are in business, do you price your products fairly or do you try to get as much as possible? Do you take advantage of people during times of famine or hardship? My wife wanted to purchase some sweaters recently so she went to the wholesale market to buy them. She was astounded to find that the price of the sweaters was 1/3 of what they were being sold for in the shops where she normally buys clothes. The shopkeepers were charging much more than enough to make a reasonable profit. They were pricing their products based on demand instead of fairness.

Another area we can mistreat others is in **charging interest.** There are many people who are very willing to lend money at extremely high interest rates. We should not be involved in such schemes, either lending or borrowing, because it is an abomination to God. A member of the church visited my office one day and poured out her story. She had borrowed money to pay for school for her children and agreed to pay very high interest, not realizing how difficult it would be. Now, she was not able to pay even the interest and her debt was growing rapidly. I felt sorry for the painful lesson she was learning and also felt anger towards the person who had taken advantage of her need.

When we lend money, we are in a position of power and we will be tempted to take advantage of that. The writer of Proverbs had some experience in this several thousand years ago when he wrote, *"He who increases his wealth by exorbitant interest amasses it for another, who will be kind to the poor."* (Prov 28:8)

The "golden rule" is the best guide for this principle, *"So in everything, do to others what you would have them do to you..."* (Mt. 7:12) Treat others the way you wish to be treated. Don't let money stop you from practicing the "golden rule."

Ask yourself, "Is there anyone that I am mistreating in my effort to make money?"

Principle Four: Be Truthful

It is very easy to try to make money by telling lies. Prov. 21:6 warns, *"A fortune made by a lying tongue is a fleeting vapor and a deadly snare."* This verse acknowledges that many do make money with lying tongues!

Lying to make money can be done in many ways. A businessman who sells goods to another will be tempted many times to directly lie to the buyer. "Oh, I just got this at the market; it is very fresh", when in reality it is a day old. A craftsman can promise, "I'll have it ready by Tuesday", but everyone knows that it won't be ready. He is afraid to tell that truth because of fear that he won't get the job. However, I believe an honest workman will always have work to do! I dealt with one carpenter who was not a Christian but he had a reputation for honesty. He would tell me openly, "I can't do that work for you until two weeks from now." Still he had customers lining up at his shop because everyone knew that he was telling the truth.

Lying can be done with dishonest weights, putting the best product on top and placing the poor quality ones where they are hidden. This sin is as old as Bible times. *"Hear this, you who trample the needy and do away with the poor of the land, saying, 'When will the New Moon be over that we may sell grain, and the Sabbath be ended that we may market wheat?' —*

skimping the measure, boosting the price and cheating with dishonest scales, buying the poor with silver and the needy for a pair of sandals, selling even the sweepings with the wheat." (Amos 8: 4-6) Does that sound like business today?

Neglecting to tell a part of the truth can also be lying. "This is a good, healthy cow at a bargain price!" What is hidden is the fact that the cow has never been able to have a calf!

Once I had a car that I wanted to sell and it had several problems. I determined that I would hide nothing from the buyer, so when he came to look at it I told him everything that was wrong with the vehicle! He was so astonished at my truthfulness that instead of bargaining to reduce the price he offered to pay me more than I was asking for the car and he happily drove it away.

If you want God's blessing on your finances, tell the whole truth. Ask yourself, "Is there any area in which I am not telling the truth in order to get money?"

Principle Five: Rest on Sunday

Another principle that will bring God's blessing in our finances is to honour the day of rest, called the Sabbath day in scripture.

Ex 31:15, *"For six days, work is to be done, but the seventh day is a Sabbath of rest, holy to the LORD. Whoever does any work on the Sabbath day must be put to death."*

Jer. 17:22, *"Do not bring a load out of your houses or do any work on the Sabbath, but keep the Sabbath day holy, as I commanded your forefathers."*

Neh. 13:15, *"In those days, I saw men in Judah treading wine presses on the Sabbath and bringing in grain and loading it on donkeys, together with wine, grapes, figs and all other kinds of loads. And they were bringing all this into Jerusalem on the Sabbath. Therefore I warned them against selling food on that day."*

These verses and many others make it clear that God has planned for you to work for six days and rest on the seventh day. It may seem like you can't afford to rest but the truth is that you can't afford not to! Too many believers leave church and then go and open their businesses, or simply employ others to run it for them!

I knew a man who was a fisherman and when he was interested in buying a big boat to fish he sought advice from many fishermen. They all told him, "If you are going to make it in this business, you must do two things: cheat on your taxes and work on Sunday." As he started his business, he told God that he would not cheat on his taxes and he would not work on Sunday. Even if he was offshore and couldn't come home on Sunday he would stop fishing and rest that day. Others, fishing around him, laughed at him and thought he was crazy. But, because he followed God's principles, he soon had a reputation in the area as the best fisherman!

My wife's parents operated a small shop near their home. They decided that they would not open on Sunday because of their understanding of scripture. Some people couldn't understand their motives and from a business perspective it was a foolish decision. Yet, they reported that they always made more on Saturday and Monday, enough to make up for shutting down on Sunday!

I realize that some professions require Sunday work, such as the medical profession. It is important then, to find another day for rest. You may also be employed in a difficult situation where your boss demands that you work on Sunday even though you don't want to work. You may try to appeal to your boss and give him a suggestion about how the work can be done in six days. Seek God's wisdom on how to handle the issue, but determine to honor God's word.

Before I leave this issue, I should also challenge those who don't work on Sunday and feel good about their obedience. But they inadvertently support those who work when they use Sunday as their day to go shopping or eat out. Think about it!

Principle Six: Avoid "get-rich-quick" schemes

"Get-rich-quick" schemes are things like sweepstakes, casinos or slot machines, special prayers to multiply your money, letters promising that a lot of money will come back to you, emails luring people into all sorts of schemes, etc. They all appeal to the desire to get rich quickly without work. The thought of instantly becoming a millionaire looks very attractive and I'm sure we've all been tempted! The Bible warns against such things.

Prov. 21:5, *"The plans of the diligent lead surely to advantage, but everyone who is hasty comes surely to poverty."*

Prov. 12:11, *"He who tills his land will have plenty of bread, but he who chases fantasies lacks judgment."*

Prov. 13:11, *"...he who gathers money little by little makes it grow."*

"Get-rich-quick" schemes appeal to selfish motives of greed and laziness. Many people fall for them because their heart is already seeking money and they have not learned contentment. When something seems too good to be true it probably is! God's plan generally is to prosper you little by little through hard work. The Swahili saying in East Africa is very true, "Kidogo, kidogo, hujaza kibaba." (Little by little fills the tin.)

What about sweepstakes or lotteries? Recognize that they both prey on people's desire to get rich quickly. They are also done as business ventures, which means that more people must buy tickets than will receive money. The odds are always in favour of the business, not the consumer! If you are lucky enough to win you will get rich at someone else's expense. They also tend to exploit the poor who can least afford it. The temptation is to buy a ticket instead of bread because maybe I will get what I need. The ground around every sweepstakes booth is littered with evidence of squandered money.

Many believers have lost money to con artists who prey on people's desires to get rich quickly. Some have allowed a con man to "pray" over their money as they left the bank promising that it would multiply! After I taught this lesson in one church a young man came to see me. He showed me a letter he had which promised that if he would "sell" the letter to several other people, he would become rich one day when thousands of people would deposit money into his bank account. It was just another variation of a get-rich-quick scheme and I advised him to get out of it. He later came and told me that he had gotten out and that most of the people he knew in the scheme didn't get their money.

Principle Seven: Give

A final principle about how we should get money seems like a contradiction: Give! Although it seems like giving will make us poorer instead of more prosperous, the Bible teaches the opposite, that giving will release blessing in our lives. Givers are blessed. *"It is more blessed to give than to receive."* (Acts 20:35)

As you work hard, treat others well and honor God's day of rest, remember to give. You should avoid the temptation to focus only on what you can get for yourself. Giving frees you from the bondage of putting your security in things and it unlocks God's blessing in your life.

Don't neglect giving. It is so important that we will look at it in more detail as the sixth key. For now, realize that giving is a principle that must be kept in focus as we earn money. A great Christian leader once said, "Earn all you can, save all you can, and give all you can."

> **"Earn all you can, save all you can, and give all you can."**

We need to recognize and obey God's plan for us to earn money. If in any area we are violating his plan, we can't expect that he is going to bless us with more.

Action Point: Take a moment and review the seven principles from this key. Ask God to change you in any areas in which you find yourself not walking in obedience to his plan for earning money. Share with someone what you are planning to change.

KEY FOUR

AVOID DEBT!

"The rich rule over the poor and the borrower is servant to the lender." (Prov. 22:7)

KEY FOUR:
AVOID DEBT

It was a tough month for Lois and Fred. School fees had eaten deeply into their pockets and by the 20th they were completely out of money. Fred approached a good friend and asked to borrow enough money to put fuel in his vehicle.

Lois begged the shopkeeper to allow her to get some items on credit until the end of the month and made arrangements with her employer to get an advance on her salary. For the moment it looked like their problems were solved. But the following month the situation worsened. After repaying the money they had borrowed, they found themselves in trouble again by the 15th. This time a loan from Fred's cooperative society helped them out and they made it through the month. But six months later they found themselves hopelessly entangled in debt with no solution in sight. Dodging creditors had become second nature to them and they had lost several friends because of failure to repay what they had borrowed.

Lois and Fred's life is typical of many couples struggling to survive from month to month. Before they knew what was happening they owed money to so many places that they almost lost track of what was happening. Think about your life right now. Do you owe anyone any money that you have not been able to pay? If your answer is yes, this key is for you! Debt is an area in which many people violate God's clear directions in scripture and are in financial bondage either through ignorance of the Bible's teaching or willful disobedience.

5 Reasons why debt is wrong

Debt violates scripture

Rom. 13:8 says very simply, *"Owe no man anything."* This is not a complicated verse! It doesn't require a deep knowledge of the Greek language to understand. It simply says that we should not owe anyone anything. How many of us can say that we don't owe anyone any money? Have you taken and not repaid; have you borrowed and not returned?

This verse may well apply to debts that we are not repaying as promised instead of any debt at all, but it is still a powerful warning for us not to be in debt. Consider what other scriptures say about debt.

Prov. 22:26, *"Do not be a man who strikes hands in pledge or puts up security for debts..."*

Ps. 37:21, *"The wicked borrow and do not repay, but the righteous give generously."*

Clearly, it is not God's will for us to be in debt.

Debt produces bondage

A second reason that debt is wrong is that it produces bondage. Solomon says, *"The rich rule over the poor and the borrower is servant to the lender."* (Prov. 22:7)

When you are in debt you are in bondage. Even when you have gone into it carefully and prayerfully you are still in bondage. You surrender a part of your freedom when you are in debt. Someone else controls a part of you. There is a certain portion of your salary that is not available for you to use in the way that you desire to use it because you owe money to someone. This is **financial** bondage.

Debt also brings bondage in **relationships**. When you owe someone money it becomes very difficult for you to continue relating to them with the same freedom that you once had. Every time you see them you are thinking about that money and it adversely affects the relationship. Countless relationships have been destroyed because of debt.

Likewise, when you loan money to someone that person becomes your slave. Even if you have given with a free heart, it will bring a tension into the relationship. I remember many times that I have tried to loan money to people thinking *this time it will work well.* Sometimes I would even forgive a debt to save the relationship and still the person would always remember that financial issue and we could not relate freely. I discovered painfully that Solomon spoke the truth. Now I refuse to lend money! If I give someone a loan it will only force that person to be my servant according to Prov. 22:7. I'd rather have a friend than a slave! So I often tell people, "If I loan you money you will become my slave. I value our friendship too much for that. I'd rather give you what little I am able than to lose our friendship."

Does this mean we can't share? Of course not! Sharing is a biblical principle that should be encouraged. There are many biblical examples of God using brothers to meet the needs of a fellow believer but asking for a loan is very different from spontaneous sharing from another. (See Acts 2:45 and 2 Cor. 8:14)

At times debt even produces **physical bondage.** Many people have ended up in jail because of debts both in Bible times and in our modern society. Mt. 18:25 gives one Biblical example. Many persons have lost their homes or businesses because of debt. The auctioneer has brought many painful memories to countless families as they watched their property being carried away. A good friend of our family called us one day in desperation. Without going into details she asked for prayer and said she would call back later. Soon we heard that she was in prison for failure to repay a loan. Naturally, this was a very painful time for her, her family, and those of us who loved her.

Debt is a sign of God's curse

In the book of Deuteronomy God gives many signs of his blessing and curses on his people. Their obedience to his commands was the determining factor in whether or not they would be blessed.

Dt. 15:6, *"You will lend to many nations, but you will not borrow."*

This was a sign of God's blessing on their lives.

Dt. 28:44, *"He shall lend to you, but you shall not lend to him. He will be the head, but you will be the tail."* This was a sign of God's curse on them.

So debt can be a sign that we are violating God's commandments. As we will see later, there may be cases in which it is right to borrow money, but generally speaking, if you have debts in your life and are not able to find a way out, it is a sign that you are under God's curse.

Debt damages God's reputation

> **When you are in debt you are in bondage**

We are God's representatives here on earth. We are his ambassadors and have already seen that we are stewards of all that we possess. We preach Phil. 4:19, *"But my God will supply all your needs according to his riches in glory..."* But what does it say when we preach this and then ask to borrow food or to borrow money?

What kind of testimony is it when we owe money at every shop? What kind of testimony is it when we can't pay our bills on time? Can you ask your landlord to receive Christ when you are behind on paying rent? Yet we speak of a God who supplies for us all our needs. WE SHAME THE NAME OF JESUS WHEN WE OWE DEBTS THAT WE ARE UNABLE TO PAY TIMELY! Believers should be walking in obedience to God's principles including financial principles and representing to the world the power of his word.

Debt shuts out the voice of God

Debt is also wrong because it allows us to ignore the voice of God in our lives. I strongly believe that God speaks to us though his provision or withholding of finances in our lives. When God provides we should move ahead. When he withholds we should do without. When we quickly go into debt we place ourselves in a position in which we cannot hear the voice of God. He may be saying that we don't need that television right now but we ignore his voice and get a loan. We enjoy hearing God say "Yes," but we can't imagine that he might say "No." Now God can no longer speak to us through finances because we have gone another route to get money instead of trusting in him alone. The God who was able to provide manna in the wilderness and clothe his people for 40 years can surely supply our needs. God didn't expect the Israelites to go to Egypt for a loan!

Paul desired to preach the gospel to the Gentiles. At one point in his ministry he worked with his hands and preached part time. When Silas and Timothy joined him he was able to resume full time ministry. Presumably, they provided finances for him to continue the ministry. Paul was able to wait on God to provide before he continued. (See Acts 18:1-5)

Many times debt keeps us from seeing the miraculous provision of God. If you have asked God to provide for school fees and he doesn't seem to be listening, it is very tempting to rush out and get a loan. *After all*, you reason, *God helps those who help themselves!* With the loan you "assist" God in providing. But perhaps his miracle was just about to come when you went for a loan! Now, you missed the miracle and are left with the debt to pay back. A family in Europe sat down for supper one evening and there was no food on the table. The children asked, "Father, where is supper?" He replied, "It has not arrived but we will give thanks for it." They bowed their heads to pray and before they said "Amen" there was a knock on the door. Someone had come and brought food to that family! What would have happened if the man had gone to the shop to buy food on credit?

One day my wife mentioned to me that she thought I should take some vegetables over to our neighbor. I said that I would do it, but didn't take immediate action. A little latter she reminded me again and insisted rather strongly that I go. I picked up the vegetables and took them over to the neighbor. Later the mother told us that she had already started cooking what little she had but she didn't have any vegetables. She told her daughter that God would provide and then I showed up at the door with exactly what they were missing!

This does not mean that it is wrong to seek assistance from friends, family or even organizations, but seek gifts rather than loans if you are in need. Make sure that you are intently following the voice of God.

For these reasons, I believe that a believer should not be in debt. It is surely a sign that we need to carefully examine ourselves and see what is happening. Before we look at solutions, let's learn more about the nature of debt.

The seductive nature of debt

Debt is a very seductive thing. It is slippery and we need to think carefully about it. I believe many believers fall in this area simply because they don't recognize the nature of debt.

Debt is easy to enter into but hard to exit

I believe that debt is deadly because it is so easy to get into, yet so hard to get out of. Borrowing money always looks attractive since it is much easier than working for it. When we borrow we can have immediately what may have taken us a long time to get through savings. Therefore, it is very attractive to us and very easy to enter. But repaying, what a different story!

My wife employed a lady to help with some jobs around the house and after a few months the lady requested a loan that amounted to about 1/3 of her monthly salary. We sat down to talk with her about it and she assured us that she would be able to easily repay the loan in three months by having us deduct money from her salary. We asked her, "Do you currently have more than enough to live on?" She responded emphatically, "Oh no, it's never enough." "Could you live on less than you are now getting?" Again she responded firmly, "No." We tried to help her see our reasoning and asked, "So, if we would pay you less would you be able to survive?" Again the response was clearly "No". "But you wouldn't have a problem repaying the loan?" "Oh, no" she responded, "That won't be a problem." She never did see what we were trying to show her. She could only see how much the loan would help her and not the difficulty of repaying.

I recently got a letter in the mail which boldly proclaimed "Your life can change in a day!" It was another offer for a loan that was supposed to change my life. I told my wife, "Sure, my life will change…I'll be in debt and have to make payments for years!" Look before you leap!

Scripture warns of the consequences when we get into a debt we cannot repay. It says in Prov. 22:26-27, *"Do not be a man who strikes hands in pledge or puts up security for debts; if you lack the means to pay, your very bed will be snatched from you."* Many have learned this lesson the hard way.

Debt quickly becomes a habit

Debt quickly becomes a habit, because the more you borrow the more you need to borrow just to maintain your life. Very quickly you will find yourself living on next month's income. A large portion of your salary is going to repay debts. Soon you feel overwhelmed and you will start to violate other scriptural principles (such as tithing or giving) to get out of trouble. This only worsens the trap and you sink further and further into despair.

I once listened to an appeal of a certain Christian brother. I was on a church committee and he wrote a letter to us asking to borrow money. He explained that with the money he got from us he would pay off a loan that he had taken from a cooperative. Then he would be eligible to apply for a bigger loan and repay us and be able to do some other things he wanted to do. So in summary he wanted a loan to repay a loan to get another loan to repay our loan and he would remain with a bigger loan! He was trapped and didn't realize it. Lord, help us!

Debt hides the real cost

Debt is seductive because it always conveniently hides the true cost. Few persons getting into debt really understand the final cost and the lender usually keeps quiet. You will hear "easy monthly installments" or "an easy payment plan". Such advertising appeals only to the short-term aspect of your finances and if you only ask, "Can I afford the monthly payment?", you will fall for the trap. The true cost comes only when you compare the cost of buying cash with the cost of credit. Hire purchase schemes also encourage us to buy more expensive items with credit than we would have even considered if we had to pay cash.

In Kenya, a television may cost 28,000 shillings cash but the store will allow you to purchase it at "only" 3737 shillings per month plus a deposit of 8000 shillings. It sounds good but in the end that TV has cost you a total of 53,020 shillings, almost twice the cash price!

Not only that, by the time you finish paying for it you have a year old TV that has almost stopped working before you have completed the payment. Take a closer look. If you would only save the same amount (3737 shillings) for less than 6 months you could pay cash for the TV and take it home with a real smile! Around the world the currency changes but the principle remains the same: debt is costly.

Loans for large purchases, such as a home, can easily cost double the borrowed amount. (One way to reduce this is to make extra principle payments on the loan that reduces the amount owed. See a financial consultant for more information on how this can help you.)

Steps to get out of debt

What can you do when you find yourself in debt? Is there any way out? Yes, there are steps that you can take to free yourself from debt! They will be painful but when you take them God will release his blessing on your life.

Deal with your heart

Allow God first of all to speak to your heart about debt. Review the passages of scripture that we have looked at in this lesson. Look at the reasons why you find yourself in debt. Is it a lack of contentment? Disobedience? These are issues of your heart. Allow God to deal with them before you move to the steps that follow.

Stop spending more than you are making

At least you can avoid getting further into debt. From today make a commitment **that if you don't have money you won't buy it!** This is a simple statement but it will radically change the way many of us live. It is better to live without things rather than purchasing on credit.

IF GOD DOES NOT PROVIDE YOU WITH THE MONEY, DON'T

DO IT! This is a strong statement and I believe it applies to food, clothing, education, and many other areas. I would rather that you don't eat supper one night than to go out to the store and ask to buy some bread on credit! Paul says, *"I have known hunger and thirst and have often gone without food; I have been cold and naked."* (2 Cor. 11:27) Surely he was tempted to borrow money to get through those difficult days. But he determined to "owe no man anything." Make a commitment today that **"I will reduce my standard of living to the level of God's provision."**

If you have been using credit cards and are entangled with them, get out the scissors and cut them into pieces.

List all your debts

Many people don't even know how far in debt they are and they probably don't want to think about it! But if you are going to be able to take control of your finances you will need to be totally honest with yourself. List all the debts you may have, from the savings cooperative to friends (and maybe some enemies!) and family. List the amount you owe, the person to whom you owe the money and, if applicable, the interest you are paying on the loan.

Make a plan for paying them

After you know what your debts are, you can begin working on a plan to repay them.

Which ones are the most important or urgent? Which ones have the highest interest? Decide which ones need attention first and decide how you will begin to repay them.

You need to look at what you have been making and spending and then decide how you are going to reduce your debts. Determine the monthly payment that you will make towards the debts and begin paying them.

This will require a lot of discipline from you because there will always be issues that come up that make it very difficult to continue with your plan. Force yourself to do it. You can do it!

Here's one tip that will make a powerful difference in the speed at which you can come out of debt. When you have decided how much of your budget to apply to debt reduction you will soon be able to clear some of the debts you have. When one debt is cleared, don't spend the additional money you now have! USE IT TO PAY THE OTHER DEBTS UNTIL THEY ARE ALL CLEARED! In this way your ability to repay will multiply as you continue and even large loans can be repaid.

Talk to your creditors

If you are serious about getting out of debt you will need to go to the people to whom you owe money and explain to them how you will repay. Most will accept your plan if they see that it is reasonable for you and that you are committed to fulfilling your promise. Don't promise more than you can realistically pay. It's better to promise little and be able to do it than to promise more than you can do. Once you have agreed on an amount, **be faithful in paying**! Take your commitment as a serious obligation before God.

Sell items to be free from debt

It is so crucial to be free of debt that I encourage you to sell some items to repay loans. It is better to sell something to pay off your loans than to remain with the item and continue suffering the bondage of being in debt. Sell the sofa set and sit on stools! You'll feel better on the stools and out of bondage than you did in the comfortable seat with debts! Look around and ask, "What do I have that I could sell to be released from debt?" I believe God will honour this if we are really serious about getting out of debt.

Some time after I taught this at one church an elder from the church came to me and reported, "After the teaching on debt, my wife and I decided to sell our car to pay off our loans!" I was stunned at his level of commitment and asked what he was going to do now. He replied that he was using public transportation until God would provide a car for the family without debt. A year later I saw him again, driving a car which was much nicer than the one he had sold! He was a free man. It was not an easy road, but well worth the sacrifice.

Save instead of borrowing

As soon as you come out of debt, start saving the same money you used to repay loans. If you are able to repay loans, then you are able to save. Saving is the opposite of borrowing and produces powerful positive results in our lives. Prov. 21:20 says, *"In the house of the wise are stores of choice food and oil, but a foolish man devours all he has."* It is wise to save. Saving will protect you from the "emergencies" that often send you looking for a loan.

Many employers offer savings schemes that make it easy for you to save. Unfortunately, most people, believers included, use them only as places to save enough to get a loan! The Christians should be loaning and let the unbelievers do the borrowing!

You may not feel that you have any excess money that you can save. Start small with whatever you can squeeze from your budget. Establish a habit and then allow it to grow.

Prov. 13:11 says, *"...He who gathers money little by little makes it grow."*

You can get out of debt. Thousands of people have discovered financial freedom by following these principles. It may take a month, or even years for you to be free but determine today that you will do whatever it takes.

Is it ever right to borrow?

There is much debate within Christian circles on whether or not it is always wrong to borrow. Romans 13:8 is clear that we should not owe anyone anything. Some interpret this verse to mean that we should not default on our obligations. Therefore, as long as we are paying our debts in a timely manner we are not in violation of this scripture. If this interpretation of Rom. 13:8 is correct, there is no clear scriptural instruction saying, "Thou shalt not borrow money." However, the scripture does clearly outline the dangers and consequences of being in debt as we have already seen and we need to take these instructions seriously and learn wisdom.

I have stated my case against debt quite strongly as I have seen it bring grief to many people and is, I believe, one of the greatest bondages in which many people are living. Having said all that, I do want to look briefly at some instances in which I believe it may be advisable to borrow money.

It might be advisable to borrow when the item is **an appreciating item** or **an item that produces income**. For example, land is generally an appreciating item that becomes more valuable over time. A business may require **a capital loan** that will eventually produce money. An **education** is an investment that will better equip us to earn income. I see these items in a very different light than borrowing to have a nicer TV, better clothes, or other items that many people borrow money in order to obtain.

Still, we must be very careful in this and make sure we are following God's plan for our lives as it will still produce a level of bondage that is inescapable with debt. Just because the borrowing looks legitimate and makes good financial sense, it still doesn't mean that God wants us to do it. Remember, we are stewards of his money and at least he should approve of what we are doing! We should not blindly follow what others are doing without seeking God's guidance and making sure that we have heard from him on this issue. We might still miss out on great miracles when we too quickly get a loan for what we want. I could tell the long story of how God provided for my family to build a house debt free. It's a story of God's provision that we will always remember as a family. At another time, I bought a house with a loan and also believe that it was his plan for us at that time.

In any case, we should make sure that we are able to easily repay the loan. If it puts too much burden on our salary we will need to wait. We should also borrow only after much prayer and obtaining wise counsel.

Following the guidelines below will save much heartache and grief when considering a loan for any of the items mentioned above:

1. Pray.

Seek God's direction. Remember you are still a steward of God's resources and you should have a clear direction from him before proceeding. Be careful that you don't just hear what you want him to say!

2. Get Godly counsel.

Talk to someone who is financially free and get advice from him or her. Reveal to that person all the details of what you want to do and allow him or her to ask you questions. Your pastor can also give you godly counsel even if he is not a businessman.

3. Don't borrow more than you can afford to lose.

Ask yourself, "What if everything fails? Could I ever repay the debt?" Do I have adequate assets at my disposal that I would be able to repay?

4. Don't borrow more than you can realistically repay.

Plan carefully how much you can afford to repay. Have you been able to live within your budget for an extended time? Are you saving money? If you doubt your ability to repay, try living for several months on the income that you would have after taking the loan. See if it actually works. Again, a godly counselor can help you to know if you are being realistic.

5. Find the best interest rates.

If you have concluded that it is right for you to take a loan then look for the best possible interest rates. Savings and loan cooperatives are often good places that charge low interest.

What about cosigning?

Cosigning, or signing as a pledge for another person, is related to borrowing because you are held legally responsible for the loan of the other person. Many people enter into this agreement without giving serious thought to the implications. They even forget that they did it until a letter arrives in the mail or a lawyer shows up at their door. This practice is strongly condemned in scripture.

Prov 6:1-5, *"My son, if you have put up security for your neighbor, if you have struck hands in pledge for another, if you have been trapped by what you said, ensnared by the words of your mouth, then do this, my son, to free yourself, since you have fallen into your neighbor's hands: Go and humble yourself; press your plea with your neighbor! Allow no sleep to your eyes, no slumber to your eyelids. Free yourself, like a gazelle from the hand of the hunter, like a bird from the snare of the fowler."*

Prov 11:15, *"He who puts up security for another will surely suffer, but whoever refuses to strike hands in pledge is safe."*

It looks clear to me. Cosigning is just as serious as getting into debt, don't do it!

Action Point: Take steps NOW, to get out of debt. Ask God's forgiveness where you have violated his principles and then take the necessary steps to get out of debt. I promise you that you will begin to see God's blessing on your finances and experience more freedom than you have dreamed possible.

KEY FIVE

LEARN TO TITHE

"Bring the whole tithe into the storehouse..."
(Malachi 3:10)

KEY FIVE:
Learn to Tithe!

Picture yourself sitting comfortably in church on Sunday morning. Your pastor, Chris, has just stood up to preach. As he begins the introduction there is a disturbance in the rear of the church. You turn around to look and find several uniformed policemen walking down the isle. They approach pastor Chris and he pauses when he sees them.

"Pastor", the officer says, "Under orders from the chief of police we have come with a warrant of arrest for 40 members of this church. Their names are listed here in this document." He hands the document to Pastor Chris. The church is deadly quiet as Pastor Chris reads through the document talking quietly to himself, "This man is one of my elders, this one is a home church leader, this one is a faithful sister who has been here for years...." His voice trails off into silence. Then he looks at the officer and says, "Really, there must be some mistake. I know these people. What have they done?"

The officer quickly replies, "They are thieves, all of them. They are being charged with robbery without violence."

"Surely there is a mistake" Chris says, "Do you have any evidence against these people?"

"Plenty" the police replies. "Just look in your own Bible at Malachi 3:8-12 and you'll see the evidence."

Pastor Chris opens his Bible to the passage and solemnly reads these words:

> *Will a man rob God? Yet you rob me. But you ask, 'How do we rob you?' "In tithes and offerings. You are under a curse—the whole nation of you—because you are robbing me. Bring the whole tithe into the storehouse, that there may be food in my house. Test me in this," says the LORD Almighty, "and see if I will not throw open the floodgates of heaven and pour out so much blessing that you will not have room enough for it. I will prevent pests from devouring your crops, and the vines in your fields will not cast their fruit," says the LORD Almighty. "Then all the nations will call you blessed, for yours will be a delightful land," says the LORD Almighty.*

After reading the text, Pastor Chris requests the officers to allow him to preach a message from the text before the culprits will be arrested. Here are the four principles he shared about tithing.

TITHING PREVENTS DISOBEDIENCE

The text says that when we fail to give our tithes and offerings we are robbing
God! This is a serious offense, robbery in the house of God! When you steal from someone else you may have the hope that you won't be discovered. Or when a thief steals from his neighbor he may do so in the hope that he will be able to bribe the policeman. But what is our hope if we are robbing God?

Malachi even says that those who fail to pay their tithes are under a curse! Why does God take this so seriously? Because failing to tithe is disobedience!

Tithing is a command

Tithing prevents disobedience because tithing is commanded in scripture. The people to whom Malachi was speaking knew the command of God given in Dt. 14:22, *"Be sure to set aside a tenth of all that your fields produce each year."* This is a simple explanation of tithing: Giving God 10% of all your income.

Any command of God is a command, not a suggestion. There is a universal principle that we need to understand: <u>when we obey a command of God our life is blessed and when we disobey we suffer.</u>

This principle does not change depending on which country you live in, what economic status you have, how much you earn, or what language you speak. It is not only for times of plenty but also for times of economic hardship. It is not only for the weeks that you have cleared your debts and paid all the bills, <u>it is a universal, timeless command of God.</u> We do not tithe because we *have*; we tithe because *it is commanded*! Commands of God are to be obeyed without question or arguing! For this reason alone we need to tithe, even if it didn't do anything for us in return.

What happens when we disobey? God doesn't treat us like a police officer who will lock us up for theft. God simply locks up his blessings and allows the natural consequences of our disobedience to follow us.

We are to tithe completely

The verse says that we are to bring the *"whole tithe"*. We are not supposed to bring part of it; we are not supposed to bring it occasionally; but we are to bring the *whole* amount.

In the Old Testament the tithe was the minimum standard for the people but actually they were expected to give far more than 10%. They were to bring tithes, offerings, and many special offerings. Many scholars believe that the total was to be nearly 20% of one's income! This may well be why the New Testament doesn't speak about the tithe; our hearts are expected to be more generous than the law required and we are expected to obey from our hearts, not just from the law.

Too many people are looking for ways to reduce their tithe, so they think, "Let me just tithe on my take-home pay." Or, "I shouldn't count that as income since my daughter got sick and I had to pay the doctor from that amount." Or you may be glad that one Sunday you can't make it to church so you don't have to give the tithe. Stop trying to bargain with God! He wants the tithe; he commands the tithe and we are to bring it completely! I believe that when we start looking for ways to "save" our tithe money we have lost sight of the goal that should be to please God and recognize his ownership of everything.

Many people argue about whether to give to God on the net or the gross income. I believe that we should give from the gross but this is not a law. Surely if you are not even paying on the net you need to start! (See *Appendix B* for more explanation)

If your income is from a business, then you should pay a tithe of the profit. This requires you to keep records and find out how much you actually make; not a bad idea just from a business perspective!

We should be careful that we think of all sources of income, especially agriculture. When we harvest, that is income. When we have sheep and goats we should also think of tithing. If your chickens lay eggs think of how to give God 10% of that income.

Paul tells the Corinthians, *"On the first day of the week, each of you should set aside a sum of money in keeping with his income, saving it up, so that when I come no collections will have to be made."* (1 Cor. 16:1,2)

"In proportion to his income" suggests that the more you make the higher percentage you should give. When God prospers us we should decide to give more of it away instead of just spending it on ourselves! If you have been faithfully giving 10% maybe God is calling you to increase to 15%.

This verse also clarifies that our giving to God should not be a spur of the moment decision made when we reach church. We should plan and prepare ahead of time with what we will come. We are to set it "aside". Take the tithe away from your other money to make sure that it makes it to the right place! The writer of Proverbs says, *"Honour the LORD with your wealth, with the firstfruits of all your crops; then your barns will be filled to overflowing, and your vats will brim over with new wine."* (Prov. 3:9,10) This scripture makes it clear that we should give God the "firstfruits" of all our crops. This means that we should give God our tithe from the first portion of our income. Take out your tithe as soon as you receive any income. If you don't do it at first it will not likely remain at the end of the month! Many persons have sincerely "planned" to give the tithe at the end of the month, but an emergency always comes up and the money is used for other purposes. The only way that works is to get the tithe out first!

Setting aside God's portion first also shows respect and honour towards

God. Don't pay all the bills and then see if there is anything remaining for God. God doesn't want our leftovers; he wants the first portion! We do not tithe because we have plenty; we tithe out of obedience to God. Some people feel that they don't get enough to tithe. Perhaps they don't have enough because they are not tithing!

A lady struggled with the issue of tithing and felt that she couldn't afford it on her meager salary. One month she told God, "I just can't afford to tithe this month, please understand." Later in the month her child got sick and she had to take her to the doctor. The bills were almost more than the mother was able to pay but she managed. Later as she prayed she heard God ask, "How did you have money to pay the doctor, but you didn't have money to tithe?" She was convicted as she realized that the amount she had spent on the doctor was more than she would have given as a tithe.

TITHING IS GOOD FOR US

Not only is tithing a command which should be obeyed, it is a command that is given for our good! Giving benefits us, not God! We do not give because God is in financial distress! God says to his people, *"....I have no need of a bull from your stall...for every animal of the forest is mine, and the cattle on a thousand hills...If I were hungry I would not tell you, for the world is mine, and all that is in it."* (Ps. 50:10-12) God is not in need of what we can give him, but we have a need to give to him! Tithing is good for us because it does at least three things for us.

Tithing develops in us the character of God

Giving reflects the character of God. *"God so loved that he gave..."* (John 3:16). Our God is a giving God. He is always eager to pour out blessings upon us. He cannot fail to give because it is a part of his nature. When we learn to tithe and give his character is formed in us.

The Bible often warns against the sins of greed and covetousness. Generous giving protects us from these sins. Tithing will help us to guard our hearts against the ever-present attraction of material things.

In our sinful nature we are not givers, but takers. We desire more for ourselves and want to accumulate the things our hearts desire. We have a receiving mentality by nature. But God's nature is giving! That's why he says, *"It is more blessed to give than to receive."* (Acts 20:35). Yet, when someone receives something he often will say, "Today I am blessed!" The blessing is not in receiving but in giving! We often look for a "helping hand", not realizing that that the Bible says, *"God loves a cheerful giver."* (2 Cor. 9:7) He delights in the person who can give cheerfully because it shows his own character in the person.

Tithing reminds us that all we have is God's

Tithing also reminds us that all that we possess belongs to God. We have examined this principle of stewardship in our second key. Consider again the following verses.

"The earth belongs to God; everything in all the world is his!" (Ps. 24:1)

"'The silver is mine and the gold is mine,' declares the LORD Almighty." (Haggai 2:8)

"You have made him (man) ruler over the works of your hands; you put everything under his feet:..." (Ps. 8:6)

All our possessions belong to God. Whatever we have— land, clothes, food, blankets, TV, radio and a sofa set, —all belong to God. He has allowed us to use them and to take care of them.

When we tithe and give back to God a part of what he has blessed us with it is a way of saying, "God I recognize that *all* I have is yours, I am just giving back to you a percentage to acknowledge that you are Lord of all." Tithing is a weekly or monthly reminder that I need to yield all of my possessions to God.

Since we are using God's property, he could demand "rent" from us. He could charge us for the use of all his possessions, including the air we breathe! Someone commented that tithing is the only "rent" he expects for the use of all his property!

Tithing produces discipline in other areas of our lives.

Tithing is also good for us because it helps us to be more disciplined in other areas of our lives, especially in our finances. The simple act of calculating our tithe helps us to be more conscious of how much we have and helps us to make a budget to live by. When we are disciplined to set aside 10 percent of our money it makes us think more carefully about how we manage the remaining 90 percent. After all, it looks like we just "lost" 10% of our income and what is left needs to be handled carefully!

When we are faithful to God's principle of tithing, we are more likely to be obedient to his word in other areas of financial management: giving, being slow to get into debt, saving, etc. Those who do not learn the discipline of tithing will likely be having other financial problems as well, not just because of disobedience and the curse that it brings, but because lack of discipline in one area encourages lack of discipline in other areas.

When we learn to be disciplined with our finances we also find that other areas of our life can be more disciplined. For example, our working habits and our use of our time may improve when we learn to tithe.

So, when your pastor preaches about tithing it is not just to increase the offerings in the church but also to encourage you to do what is best for your life!

TITHING PROVIDES FOR THE WORK OF GOD

Although scripture is clear that God doesn't *need* our money, it is equally clear that he uses our tithes and offerings to accomplish his work in this world. God says through Malachi, "Bring the whole tithe into the storehouse, that there may be food in my house." God wants his house to have food for his workers and his ministries and he plans for this to be provided by his people.

The place of tithing is to the storehouse

Malachi tells us where we are to bring our tithe: to the "storehouse". In the Old Testament the storehouse was simply the storage rooms of the temple sanctuary. The people were to bring their tithes to the place of worship.

I believe that the right place to bring our tithes today is to the **local**

church where we belong. It is the local church that feeds you spiritually and it is the local church that you should support financially. When you give it does not mean that you support everything that the pastor is doing, because you are not really giving it to the church; you are giving it to God. You only give to God through the local church. But I believe that God's plan is for you to be committed to a local church and to support that church with your tithes and offerings.

It is good to give to other needs, organizations, ministries or the poor; but we are to bring the tithe to the storehouse. Add other giving to places of your choice but don't neglect the local place where you worship.

Many people don't tithe in their local church because they don't "feel" comfortable with all that is happening in the church. They attend but are not wholeheartedly willing to support the church. This is a serious problem that needs correction. Jesus says, *"For where your treasure is, there your heart will be also."* (Mt. 6:21) Many people's heart is not with their church because they have not put their money in the church. Our heart follows our money! Giving your tithe produces a powerful spiritual bond between you and your church.

Many believers also feel that this issue of tithing is just between them and God and is none of the pastor's business. I think that this is an issue of accountability to spiritual authority. If you entrust your spiritual life to the pastor, why don't you want him to know if you are tithing? Or is it because you don't want him to know what you are earning? I don't think tithing was a secret in the Bible times. In fact it was open for anyone to see what people brought to the priest. Jesus was able to observe people bringing their offerings. (Mk. 12:41-44) Be accountable to your pastor! Let him know that your heart is with the church. I often teach pastors and I tell them that they should know that their leaders are tithing. I told the leaders in my church that I expected them to tithe and if they weren't willing that they should resign from leadership. And I checked to make sure they were doing it! I know some will not agree with that but I don't believe that leadership should be given to people who have not shown that they are wholeheartedly committed to the church and to the pastor of the church.

> **Our heart follows our money!**

The purpose of tithing is to provide

God says, "Bring the whole tithe into the storehouse, that there may be food in my house." His purpose for tithes is to provide for the work of the church. According to Larry Burkett, the "storehouse" had four functions: to feed the Levites and priests; to feed the prophets; to feed the widows and orphans within Israel; and to feed the widows and orphans outside Israel. The Levites and priests would be our modern day pastors and other church staff. The prophets might be equivalent to evangelists and missionaries of today. The needs of widows and orphans have not changed with time. God clearly wanted the tithes and offerings to be used to provide for the leaders and the most needy in the society.

The church has financial needs that will be met when you are faithful in tithing. The budget at the beginning of the year is made in faith that God will enable you to tithe faithfully. God plans to meet the needs of your church through your tithe. You give because it is a command of God and his blessing will be upon the local church where God uses that money for the extension of his kingdom.

Some people refuse to tithe because they feel that the pastor should "live by faith." They obviously haven't studied the word of God! It is very biblical to support your pastor. Carefully consider the following verses:

1 Tim. 5:17-18, *"The elders who direct the affairs of the church well are worthy of double honor, especially those whose work is preaching and teaching. For the Scripture says, 'Do not muzzle the ox while it is treading out the grain,' and 'The worker deserves his wages.'"*

Galatians 6:6, *"Anyone who receives instruction in the word must share all good things with his instructor. Do not be deceived: God cannot be mocked. A man reaps what he sows."*

1 Cor. 9:14, *"In the same way, the Lord has commanded that those who preach the gospel should receive their living from the gospel."*

Several principles can be drawn from these verses:

1. It is right for the worker to eat from the work. Some people complain that the pastor is "eating" the money. He's supposed to eat it!

Everyone eats from the work of his or her hands. Why do we think it is degrading for a man of God to receive his income from the church? Paul even suggests that they are worth a higher salary when he talks of "double honor". Why should the manager of a company with 200 employees receive more than a pastor who oversees the spiritual welfare of 500 members? Of course, this is not to excuse the misuse of money by church leaders. They will account to God for how they handle the money given by the people. However, that is another topic altogether.

2. It is right for those who are ministered to spiritually to give material things (money) to the minister. The "good things" Paul refers to is not a casual, "God bless you, pastor!" He's talking about giving material support.

3. Only the minister has the right to refuse this support. It is not the right of the people to refuse to give it. When a minister does it, he should have a good reason and do it for a limited time only or it will be detrimental to his life and the life of the people as the experience of the apostle Paul demonstrates.

4. The manner in which people pay their leaders brings spiritual fruit in their own lives. The law of sowing and reaping is not a message to sinners telling them to repent of the evil seeds they have sown. It is a message to the church that they should not be foolish in the way they give to support the minister!

The way that they sow into his life will determine what God will give to them. Reflect on that for a few minutes!

Is it clear yet? God expects his ministers to be supported—not by faith, but by the people of faith!

The Old Testament is filled with examples of how God expected the people to provide for the priests and Levites. Time after time the nation of Israel rose and fell on this principle…as soon as the people stopped supporting the ministers, the priests would go back to their fields; the work of God would be neglected and sin would continue to increase. With revivals, there was always an accompanying increase in the support of the ministry and the priests returned to their duties. (See 2 Chr. 30-31 for one example.)

Many pastors suffer needlessly because they are ashamed to teach their people about finances. It is a difficult subject to teach about and the pastors should examine their motives before doing so, but recognize that it is God's plan that the church should support workers in the church. Paul apologized to the church in Corinth for failing to demand that they support him. Ironically, while he was trying to show love them, they didn't even respect his apostleship. He says to them, *"How were you inferior to the other churches, except that I was never a burden to you? Forgive me this wrong!"* (2 Cor. 12:13) The only time he apologized to a church was to say that he regretted not expecting them to support him!

> God expects his ministers to be supported— not by faith, but by the people of faith!

While most churches suffer a lack of finances, I am sure that this is not God's plan. If God's people would be faithful in giving their tithes and offerings, God's workers would have plenty and the work would go on well.

TITHING PRODUCES EVIDENCE OF GOD'S FAITHFULNESS

The third key principle that Malachi teaches us is that when we tithe God will show his faithfulness. In fact, the message seems to be that God is just waiting for us to do our part so that he can do what he promises.

"Test me in this," says the LORD Almighty, "and see if I will not throw open the floodgates of heaven and pour out so much blessing that you will not have room enough for it."

We are challenged to test God with tithing

God gives us a challenge, a dare to do something. There is no other place in scripture where God openly challenges us to test him and see if he will do as promised. But here, he asks us to try him.

Satan will give us many excuses about why we shouldn't give to God, but God says, "Test me!" What are you waiting for? What more do you need? God will never be in debt to anyone, nor will he ever fail. Many believers have not really believed in this part of God's faithfulness and they have never put him to the test.

Go ahead; take his challenge! Decide today that for the next six months you will faithfully tithe from all your income. Then take a look at your life and see if God has shown himself faithful. You will never experience his blessings until you are obedient to his commands. My wife and I have tithed for as long as we can remember and can tell many stories of God's faithfulness to meet our needs.

God promises blessing to those who will tithe

God says that when you test him with tithing he will "throw open the floodgates of heaven and pour out so much blessing that you will not have room enough for it." God promises blessing for those who will tithe, even more than we can imagine! God loves to give and when you start giving to him it just stimulates his giving nature and he continues giving and giving.

> **You will never experience his blessings until you are obedient to his commands**

Is this a magic formulae that if we give a certain amount we will receive twice as much the next week? Many people preach as if this will automatically happen. This may happen as God blesses us but I don't think it should be our motive. Our motive should be obedience to the word of God and a desire to grow in the character of God. When we do this we can expect to see the blessings of God because he has promised it. This blessing may come in many ways and at various times. We may find that our expenses are reduced; we may receive an unexpected bonus at work; or a friend may bring food that stretches our food budget. We may be repaid in non-material ways as well, with great joy and contentment that we never had before. We cannot demand that God fulfill his promise on our terms but we can trust that he will fulfill it because he cannot lie.

Many churches also give tithes or some form of support to their headquarters. I believe that the same principles of blessing apply to the church that is faithful in giving this support. Once at the church where I was the pastor, we found that we were not meeting our budget. The giving of the members was unexplainably low. The church council discussed the issue and discovered that we were not being faithful in giving to the headquarters as we had agreed. We rectified the problem immediately and without any other explanation the giving in the church the following month was the highest ever!

TITHING PREVENTS DESTRUCTION

A final principle that Malachi teaches us is that when we tithe God will prevent destruction in our lives.

I will prevent pests from devouring your crops, and the vines in your fields will not cast their fruit," says the LORD Almighty. "Then all the nations will call you blessed, for yours will be a delightful land," says the LORD Almighty.

The verse is clear that tithing prevents destruction. God promised his people that if they would tithe, he would take care of their source of income. He would prevent pests and disease from their fields.

The promise is still good for us today. When we are faithful to God he may simply keep some "destroyers" away from us. We may not know what accident or sickness was coming because God prevented it. When we tithe, God protects us.

The verse also implies that when we fail to tithe the opposite is true. The devil can also find ways to "steal" the 10% that belongs to God. Many times problems come to us because we have been unfaithful in giving. Many times our business can lose money or our children can get sick just because we are not tithing. We should not call *every* sickness a result of not tithing but we need to be aware that the devil has a lot of plans for that 10%.

Action Point: Ask yourself, "Am I being faithful in the area of tithes?" Make a commitment right now to begin being faithful. Take a few minutes to talk to God about it. Then share your commitment with someone who can hold you accountable. If you are married, you may need to discuss this with your spouse and decide together to begin tithing. If you are already tithing, is God calling you to a higher level of giving?

Key Six

LEARN TO GIVE

"God loves a cheerful giver." (2 Cor. 9:7)

Key Six:
Learn to Give

There are only two kinds of people in the world: Givers and Takers. Some people are always searching for what they will receive; others look for ways to give to others. Which kind of person are you?

We have already seen that giving is one of the clear teachings of scripture. Now let's look more carefully at this important issue as our sixth key. Scripture has so much to say about giving that we won't be able to look at this subject comprehensively but we will examine three elements of giving.

THE BLESSINGS OF CHRISTIAN GIVING

It is a blessing when we give. Most people see receiving as a blessing but the Bible teaches that we are blessed when we give. Why? There are at least three reasons why it is a blessing to give.

Giving reflects the character of God

God is a giving God. "God so loved…that he *GAVE*…" He demonstrates his love with the action of giving. He gives and gives and gives. God gives life, breath, strength, beauty, air, water, flowers, friends, food, sunshine, rain, salvation, forgiveness, love, acceptance…and on and on! There is no end to the list of things that God gives you. You might say that it is because he has so much that he gives so much. But he gives not because of what he has; he gives because it is his nature to give. God gave his only son, the most costly gift ever given. God is a giver; not a taker!

Our human nature is to want to receive. We are born with loud demands for someone to meet our needs! God's nature is to give. OUR CHRIST LIKENESS IS QUICKLY REVEALED IN OUR WILLINGNESS TO GIVE. And we don't give to get. Some give at fundraisings to get their name in the paper or to impress people; but giving that reflects the nature of God is done as an act of love to the recipient.

> **There are only two kinds of people in the world: Givers and Takers**

True Christian giving is not something that we can manufacture for ourselves, or force ourselves to do; it is a manifestation of God's special work in our hearts. The closer we come to God the more we reflect his nature and our God is a giving God. It is no wonder then, that *"God loves a cheerful giver."* (2 Cor. 9:7). God loves a giver because the giver reflects his own nature. Givers are happy people. It is fun to be a giver! The "takers" are always looking for someone to give to them and always complaining that they have not been given enough. Being around such a person is a tiring experience. But spend some time with a giver; what a different experience! They experience life to the full. They are living, not for themselves, but for others. As a result, they are loved and appreciated by others. Rev. J. Maxwell says, "Giving is the highest level of living." This is because we are like God when we give.

Giving results in blessing for the giver

Paul reports the well-known words of Jesus, *"It is more blessed to give than to receive."* (Acts 20:35) Although we often quote this verse, do we really believe it? When someone receives a surprise cash gift, he will often say, "Today, I'm blessed!" But Jesus says that the person who is really blessed is the *one whogave* the gift!   If you want to experience God's blessings, GIVE!

Consider the following verses...

Prov. 28:7, *"He who gives to the poor will lack no good thing."*

Prov. 22:9, *"A generous man will himself be blessed, for he shares his food with the poor."*

Prov. 11:25, *"A generous man will prosper; he who refreshes other will himself be refreshed."*

Lk. 6:38, *"Give and it will be given to you."*

All these verses show clearly that the key to receiving is not keeping and hoarding for ourselves, but giving what we have! How often we try to have by keeping instead of trusting God as we give.

Those who give receive the joy of giving. When people are giving gifts to one another, I like to watch the person who gave the gift instead of the person who is unwrapping the present. That person's eyes always sparkle with the joy that only givers experience.

Givers bring blessing to others

When someone gives to another person a need is met in their lives and it is counted as a great blessing. Paul told the Corinthians, *"This service that you perform is not only supplying the needs of God's people but is also overflowing in many expressions of thanks to God. Because of the service by which you have proved yourselves, men will praise God for the obedience that accompanies your confession of the gospel of Christ, and for your generosity in sharing with them and with everyone else."* (2 Cor. 9:12-13)

When you give you are blessing someone else. The need in their life is met and in that sense they are also blessed. They will thank God for you and for what you have done! What a privilege to be a blessing to others. Everyone wins!

THE DIRECTION OF CHRISTIAN GIVING

Where do we give? Scripture provides two primary places to which we are to give.

Give to God

The first place that we give is to God. Since God owns everything, He doesn't need our money but we need to give! God says in Ps. 50:12, "If I were hungry I would not tell you, for the world is mine, and all that is in it." So we don't give to God because he is poor; we give to obey and honour him. We show honour to him when we give to him, just as people honour a great leader by coming to him with gifts. Giving to God helps us to keep our lives in focus and to remember who He is and who we are.

Prov. 3:9-10 instructs, *"Honor the LORD with your wealth, with the firstfruits of all your crops, then your barns will be filled with overflowing, and your vats will brim over with new wine."*

Don't think that you can withhold giving to God and prosper. It may look like the money that you put in the tithes and offering means that you will have less to live on. But in fact the opposite is true; if you fail to give you will suffer loss. GIVING IS A KEY TO UNLOCK GOD'S BLESSING IN YOUR LIFE!

Although God doesn't need our money, our money is useful to the work of the church and His kingdom. When we give to him we are giving to extend the kingdom through the church and Christian ministries. Therefore, we should not give grudgingly, but with a cheerful heart, knowing that we are storing up for ourselves treasures in heaven by investing in his work. We need to move beyond a tithe and be eager to give more to allow God's kingdom to expand. When we give to missions the kingdom of God is extended. When we give for a student to be trained in Bible School we are investing in the future. When we give to a pastor he is encouraged to continue the ministry to which God has called him.

Give to the poor

We are also to give to the poor. The scripture abounds with references to giving to the poor, showing God's concern for their lives. Look at these verses from Proverbs:

"He who gives to the poor will lack nothing, but he who closes his eyes to them receives many curses." (Prov. 28:27)

"A generous man will prosper; he who refreshes others will himself be refreshed." (Prov. 11:25)

"He who is kind to the poor lends to the LORD, and he will reward him for what he has done." (Prov. 19:17)

This is the word of God. You can ignore it to your own peril or you can decide to obey. It is clear that we are expected to give generously to those in need. You might think that you are poor because you know all the needs that you have. But you can always find someone who is needier than you are. You can bless them by giving.

THE PRINCIPLES OF CHRISTIAN GIVING

Paul wrote to the church at Corinth and challenged them in the area of giving using the example of the Macedonian churches. His words still have much to teach us about how to give.

"And now, brothers, we want you to know about the grace that God has given the Macedonian churches. Out of the most severe trial, their overflowing joy and their extreme poverty welled up in rich generosity. For I testify that they gave as much as they were able, and even beyond their ability. Entirely on their own, they urgently pleaded with us for the privilege of sharing in this service to the saints. And they did not do as we expected, but they gave themselves first to the Lord and then to us in keeping with God's will. So we urged Titus, since he had earlier made a beginning, to bring also to completion this act of grace on your part. But just as you excel in everything—in faith, in speech, in knowledge, in complete earnestness and in your love for us— see that you also excel in this grace of giving." (2 Cor. 8:1-7)

Let's look at 5 principles from this scripture about Christian giving.

Principle One: Christian giving is not related to position

Paul tells about the rich generosity of the Macedonian church. They gave generously. We easily assume that in order to *give* a lot one needs to *have* a lot. But notice what happened in the Macedonian Churches. They were not rich; they were poor! Not only was the church in poverty, but "extreme" poverty and in the midst of a "most severe trial." That doesn't seem like fertile ground for generous giving! But in their case it produced generosity. How did this happen? Paul gives us an equation that we need to look at carefully.   In mathematics we learned equations such as: 1 + 1 = 2. Here is the equation Paul gives for successful Christian giving:

Trial + poverty + joy = Generosity!

Wow! What is happening in these people? What makes them generous? Is it what they have? No, Paul indicates that it is joy that was the key for the Macedonians. Joy is not a condition of how much we have; it is an attitude. We can choose our attitude! The Macedonians clearly teach us that the amount that is given is not determined by the amount one has but by the attitude one has. What a challenge! When we expect a lot to be given we normally look to the rich. But this church gave in spite of their poverty and they enjoyed it! Christian giving is not so much a matter of ability but availability. A lot of what is given by believers does not come from the pockets of the wealthy, but from those of average means who give generously. Some of the most generous people I know are not wealthy by the standards of the world, but they have learned to be givers. On several occasions I have been a visitor in homes where I was served chicken. I knew that this chicken was a precious commodity in that family, but no one complained. They were happy to give! I felt deeply humbled in the presence of such generosity.

If we are going to give out of poverty and trials we must be creative. It was not possible for the Macedonian churches to go to the bank and make a withdrawal; there was no money in the bank! How can we give when in poverty? We need to look seriously at what God has given us and think of ways to give.   When cash is in short supply look at other ways to get things to give.

Sometimes we can do without something to save money. We can do without a newspaper or a meal. We can do without a new dress or sofa set. The money saved can be given. We can make a promise to give by faith and ask God to provide from unexpected sources. Maybe someone owes you money and unexpectedly pays it back. Now you have money to give! Perhaps your employer finds that you have been underpaid and corrects the amount. You have money to give. At other times we can sell items that we have in order to have money to give. A shirt or coat, a sofa or radio can be sold or donated. A chicken, sheep or cow can be sold to get cash. At times material items can simply be given to people in need. You have a shirt or dress that you haven't worn for months. Give it away! Look around your house and I can assure you that if you really want to give you will find something that you can give. I recall a time that our church was raising money and I wanted to contribute but didn't have much cash. I looked around and found a camera that I was no longer using and decided that I could give that. It was auctioned and brought more than I would have given in cash!

We can also plan ways in which to give. We may dedicate a portion of our farm to the Lord and whatever comes from it goes to a special project. We may set aside an animal and tell God that the firstborn from that animal will be given to him. There are many ways to give if we are creative. The Macedonians found ways to give because they wanted to give. You can do it too!

Principle Two: Christian giving comes from the heart

Christian giving is not a mechanical matter. It is not something that needs to be forced. Christian giving comes from the heart. Look again at the Macedonian churches.

They gave with joy

The key in the equation above is JOY. If joy is removed from this equation you will have dependency. But with joy in their hearts those who could be "needy cases" become givers. Joy comes from knowing our God and trusting in him to provide. It is not based on what we have; it is a choice that we make in our minds. When our trust is in God's provision and we aren't worried about tomorrow, we can be released to give joyfully. Joy is free! It is a fruit of the Spirit of God and can grow in our lives.

God loves a cheerful giver (2 Cor. 9:7). We should give with joy! Our time of giving in the church or in a fundraising event should be cheerful times! Don't give out of embarrassment, or compulsion; **give with joy**! It is fun to give. If you will take some time going through your house looking for things that you can give away you'll be surprised at how fun it is once you decide to release those items. Givers are joyful people.

> # It is fun to give!

I remember one time when I was teaching this principle in a rural church. I was dressed in a suit and tie and as I preached I decided that I could give my tie away. So as I talked about how much fun it is to give, I took off my tie and tossed it to someone in the audience. The person who was interpreting for me also took off his tie and gave it away and we both had fun!

They "pleaded" to give

Here there was no compulsion. They were pleading to give! Imagine, people coming running to give even before the sermon is finished!

Be careful in times of giving and fundraisings not to adopt the pattern of the world; to force people to give. You should not resort to tricks and manipulation. Think about the last fundraising event you attended. Were people eager to give or were they enticed to give? Good-natured humour or competition is good to provoke people to give but make sure that they are not feeling forced to give. If people aren't willing they have a heart problem—not a money problem!

In a related passage Paul says, *"Each man should give what he has decided in his own heart to give, not reluctantly or under compulsion."*

(2 Cor. 9:7) God's plan is for us to have a generous heart and then to give generously. It also implies that each of us will give differently according to how God has blessed us *and* according to the condition of our heart. Christian giving respects our individuality and doesn't force us all to give the same amount. It is fine for a church to issue a guideline or suggested standard to challenge people. But recognize that everyone is at a different level of ability and attitude.

Principle Three: Christian giving benefits the saints

Paul says that the giving of the Macedonian church was a service *"to the saints."* (v. 4) Paul says to the church at Galatia, *"Therefore, as we have opportunity, let us do good to all people, especially to those who belong to the family of believers."* (Gal. 6:10) Although it is good to give outside the church, much of our giving will be to benefit our brothers and sisters in Christ. Christian giving is a special joy because we are giving to help a part of the body of Christ. The Macedonian church was not building their own building; they were giving to send money to meet the needs of fellow believers who lived far away. There was a need among their brothers in Christ and they responded generously to meet that need.

When we give to a fellow believer it is just like giving to a brother or sister. We are helping someone who is a part of the same family. I remember a time when we held a fundraising for a church leader who had accumulated a large medical bill. As we gave I realized with joy that I was giving to bless a child of God. My giving allowed him to continue doing the work God had called him to do in the kingdom. I was investing some of my treasure in a kingdom brother. I can't take my money to heaven but I can invest it in others who are going there!

When you give you become a blessing to someone else. When you give for missions you are giving to bring more saints into the kingdom. When you give to build a church you are blessing the saints. Your regular giving enables the local church to continue serving the saints.

Principle Four: Christian giving can be improved.

Paul challenges them to, "Excel in giving." (v. 7) All we have learned leads to this point. Paul is saying that in the area of giving we can grow. It is something that we can learn to do better. We can increase. Just as we can increase in faith, we can increase in generosity.

If we are going to excel in something it means we must think about it, pray about it, practice it and learn more about it so that we can do better. We need more teaching and more challenges to learn better ways of giving. We need to improve. Let's aim to be givers like the Macedonians were. They had reached a high level of giving.

I believe that there are different levels of giving which are illustrated by the many types of offerings in the Old Testament. One such passage is Dt. 12:6, which mentions the following kinds of giving: Burnt offerings, sacrifices, tithes, special gifts, what you have vowed, and freewill offerings.

Level One: Giving which benefits the giver

Several of these offerings that were given benefited the giver. With some of the sacrifices a portion would be eaten by the priest and then he would return a portion to the one who brought the sacrifice. The worshipper would go and enjoy roasted meat with his family! It is not so hard to give when you are going to eat! This seems to be the lowest level of giving: Giving that benefits the giver.

Level Two: Giving which indirectly benefits the giver

Some types of giving don't benefit me directly but they do indirectly. Some of the Old Testament offerings were given to benefit the priests and the work of the temple. This giving enabled the temple to function which was a benefit to all the people.

Some of the special gifts, vowed gifts and freewill offerings went for the support or building of the temple. While the giver didn't "eat" from these gifts he benefited indirectly in that his needs were being served. In a similar manner today we give to the church so that the pastor can be supported. In turn, he feeds us spiritually and helps build the church. As I write we are in the midst of a major building programme in my church. We are making a great effort to give the money needed to raise that project.

Yet, at the completion of the construction who will enjoy the building? We will! When we give to build our church we will also enjoy sitting in the new sanctuary! We are the ones who will admire it and tell our friends, "Look at the church we built!" All of these are good forms of giving and need to be cultivated in our lives. However, there are higher levels.

Level Three: Giving which benefits others

The Macedonians illustrate this level of giving. They were giving to help needy believers in Jerusalem, people that they had probably never met and would not see until they reached heaven. It was not likely that those who received the money would even send them a card of thanks or a photo of how the money was used.

We can come closer to this type of giving when we give to another church that is not our local church; to places where we will never visit, or to mission work in places where we will never be known. This level of giving requires a deep love for others and a willingness to give without the applause of others. Many believers struggle to give at this level. When asked to help build a distant church they ask, "Why should I give for them?" They struggle to give money to the church headquarters thinking, *What does the Bishop do for me?* These questions indicate a level two giver.

It is good to raise money for your church building. It will be a blessing to you and it will send a good message to the community. You should give for that. It is not for unbelievers to build the church but for us who are believers. But don't stop with your church building! Continue to give and raise money to send missionaries out. Raise money to support the diocese or larger church. Give money to another denomination. Raise money to support a Bible school. Raise money to send a child to school. Give money to send to Christians in a neighboring country who don't have food to eat. That is true Christian giving; giving without expecting to benefit from it personally.

Level Four: Giving which benefits only God.

The highest level of giving seems to be the burnt offering. It was an animal given to be consumed by fire, a sacrifice only to the Lord. In this sacrifice the worshipper would bring a sheep or goat to the priest. The priest would slaughter it and then place it on the fire where it would be totally consumed. No one benefited from it! It wasn't eaten, and it could not build the temple. It was simply a sacrifice of love and honour to God. Mary gave in this way to Christ when she poured perfume on his feet. (Jn. 12:3) How much would we give in the offering if we knew that at the end of the service the pastor would take the offering basket, place it on the floor and light it with a match?

How can we give at this level? I haven't found a way to give my money directly to God, so I think this is more of a heart issue. There have been times when an offering was being taken and my heart was full of gratitude to God. I wasn't so concerened about what was going to happen to the money, I just gave out of love for God and whispered to him as I placed it in the basket, "Lord, you are so good to me...I just want to express my appreciation to you with this gift." At that point I am not giving to a cause, but to my God, needing nothing in return.

Which level are you on? Do you desire to grow to a higher level? You can learn to "excel" in giving. Perhaps you have been giving your tithe and have been contented with that. But look beyond the tithe to other ways that you can give. Of all the offerings, the tithe seems to be the only one that is directly related to income; the others were given out of their wealth or their possessions. (In the Old Testament society that was largely agricultural, most of their giving would come from their fields. In our society much of what we give comes from our income from employment.)

> You can learn to "excel" in giving

I believe that we can look much beyond our monthly pay to other areas in which God has blessed us. Many of us have land, animals, clothes, furnishings in our homes and many other things that we possess. We can look at all of them as potential resources to give. If we are to excel in giving we need to go far beyond the tithe of our income.

As we grow in the area of giving we will eventually be characterized as a giving church, just as the Macedonian church. What a beautiful thing to characterize a local church, a church that gives! Pray that this will characterize your life and your church.

Give, Give, Give! Become a Christian giver, excelling in the art of giving. Give joyfully from a heart that has been loosened from the grip of greed and responds in joyful obedience to a giving God!

Action Point: This week take a walk around your house, looking for things that you can give away. Find something that has value to you and decide to give it away. Have fun!

KEY SEVEN

Manage Finances in the Home

"If a man does not know how to manage his own family, how can he take care of God's church?"
(1 Tim. 3:5)

KEY SEVEN:
MANAGE FINANCES IN THE HOME

"What do you mean, 'There's no money'? I'm sick and tired of your excuses and I don't know what you do with all the money. The children are home because of school fees, we don't have money for food and all you can say is, 'There's no money'!"

Does this frustrated wife's outburst sound familiar? When is the last time you and your spouse had a disagreement over finances? If you're normal it was probably sometime since you began reading this book!

Home is the place where financial principles are the most severely tested. Finances are a common source of frustration and conflict between a husband and a wife. In this final section, we want to learn what God has to say about finances in the home. All of the principles we have looked at will be applied in the home but here we want to focus specifically on three Biblical principles of finances that apply in our homes.

FINANCES SHOULD BE HANDLED ACCORDING TO GOD'S PLAN

The writer of Proverbs says, *"Trust in the LORD with all your heart and lean not on your own understanding; in all your ways acknowledge him, and he will make your paths straight."* (Prov. 3:5-6). This verse makes it clear that we should not rely on our own understanding of what is right and wrong. We must rely on God's clear instruction. Yet, we often rely on other things when it comes to dealing with finances in the home.

We might follow our **culture**. "Everyone else does it this way." "My parents did it this way." These common thoughts will keep us from following the commands of scripture. Many times our culture is good but when it conflicts with the word of God we must accept that God's way is right. He created us and he knows what works well and what doesn't work at all. When we become Christians we align ourselves with the kingdom of God that is higher than any cultural or family tie which I might have. We take on a new culture and our desire should be to learn all that God's culture says about how to handle money.

Take time to read the word of God. Meditate on the scriptures used in this book and in the appendix. Many people struggle with finances simply because they don't know what God's word says about how to handle money. Make a decision now that if God says it, that settles it and you will obey it!

We might follow our **instincts**. At times we simply do what "feels" right. We look at an issue, roll it around in our minds, and propose a solution that seems right to us.

The Bible warns strongly about this step. *"All a man's ways seem right to him, but the LORD weighs the heart."* (Prov. 21: 2) Just because it "seems" right doesn't mean that it is right!

We might follow our **tradition**. "I've always done it this way." "It has always worked before." Yes, you might have always done it that way but you might be consistently wrong! Tradition often keeps us from considering change which can lead to growth.

Simply put, if we are going to experience God's blessing in our homes we must **determine to follow God's plan**. We must do it whatever the cost, however illogical it may seem, however it may conflict with our culture or tradition. When we make this decision we have taken a giant step.

Both the husband and wife should agree to follow God's plan. The principles outlined in this book can be a useful starting place for a study of God's word concerning finances. If both partners are committed to follow God's way, change can begin in the home. If necessary, get counsel from your pastor or a godly couple to help you through difficult issues.

FINANCES SHOULD BE HANDLED TOGETHER.

Finances in the home are not an issue for the husband only; nor for the wife alone. In order for the home to function as God intended it to function, financial matters must be handled by both the husband and wife. This is a general principle that is violated in many homes. Yet it is based on the most basic principle of marriage, oneness or unity. When God established marriage he said, *"For this reason a man will leave his father and mother and be united to his wife, and they will become one flesh."* (Gen. 2:24)

> **Financial matters must be handled by both the husband and wife.**

Becoming one flesh refers to much more than the physical union between a husband and a wife. It means that in all things in life they become one. A new relationship is formed. The husband and wife become partners in life. They become one. Whatever he has becomes hers and what she has becomes his. Their physical property, their bodies, and their names become one. There is nothing of which it can rightly be said, "This is his" or "That is hers."

Unfortunately, many homes don't treat finances as a partnership. The husband acts as the banker, treasurer, auditor, clerk and controller! The wife many times doesn't even know how much the husband is earning or what happens to the money. He just reports, "There's no money."

Men, if you are in a business with partners, can you make a financial decision without consulting them? Of course not! Why then in our homes do we as men feel that we can make all the financial decisions without our wives? Did we forget that *"...A prudent wife is from the Lord."*? (Prov. 19:14) God has given us a wonderful partner to share life with and in most cases the wife is very sensitive on financial issues. Many men have made disastrous mistakes financially which could have been avoided if only they would have consulted their wives. The biblical command for the wife to submit doesn't give the husband a mandate to ignore her! Neither does it mean that she can't think properly about finances. In some cases the wife is better than the husband at handling the money! It is a wise husband who will allow that partner to help the family in that way.

I was teaching this principle one time to a group of teachers. After I finished, a man stood up to ask a question. He seemed agitated as he asked, "You taught that we should be partners. But in a partnership, don't both people bring something to the table?" It took me a moment to realize that he was married to a wife who was not employed and therefore he felt like she had not contributed anything to the family. For a moment I was angry at such an attitude towards his spouse. But I quickly asked God to give me wisdom and then asked him if his wife brought anything to their family even if it was not material things. I was saddened to realize that because this man didn't see his wife as his partner, they would never enjoy the deep relationship God intended for their marriage. I was much more encouraged by a church leader who read my booklet and reported to me, "After reading the *7 Keys of Financial Freedom*, I have started talking with my wife about financial management in our family and made a budget. My wife will be our treasurer from next month." Knowing that he came from a tradition in which wives were treated like property made his statement all the more significant and I realized that he had allowed the word of God to change his life.

What can we do to apply this principle in our homes?

Discuss together

The hiding that was a result of sin in the Garden of Eden also affected financial transparency. Before the fall, Adam and Eve were open, honest, and naked with each other, physically, emotionally and in every part of life. They could talk about anything. Adam was clearly the leader but he saw Eve as a marvelous helper and partner. He wanted to know her thoughts and she helped him make wise decisions. However, as soon as sin entered the world they started "covering up". They started hiding from God and from each other.

This hiding continues in many homes today. Instead of openness there is often secrecy and darkness. Many wives don't know the full details of their husbands' income or assets. The wife finds a way to secretly save money for a special project without telling her husband. Separate bank accounts are operated privately.

In some cases this separation comes because there is a lack of legal security in the home. The wife may fear that if the husband dies she will lose anything that is not in her name. So she insists on her own bank account and keeps another private box under the bed. The husband can help ease this fear in several ways. He should **write a will** clearly stating his desires in case of death. This perhaps will go against culture but will save a lot of grief in the event of his early death. If possible he can **purchase life insurance**. He should also **communicate well with his extended family** about his wife so that they know clearly that what belongs to him belongs to both of them together. He should insure that **all title deeds** and important documents **bear both of their names**. This can prevent terrible tragedies in case of the death of the husband. This is an important part of the man protecting his wife. We have all heard stories of what happens to some wives after their husband's death. Family members come like vultures and take everything that they can get their hands on. A Christian husband should do all he can to prevent this tragedy.

If you have not been discussing finances with your wife, it is time to start. Tell her your salary, tell her about any investments you have, tell her if you have life insurance, etc. She is your partner; don't hide anything from her. Likewise, wives, if you have not been open with your husband start today!

If you have been maintaining separate bank accounts join them together or at least bring the accounts out into the open. You are one!

Both of you should be aware of the financial status of the family at all times. When the wife needs money for food and the husband replies without explanation, "There's no money," the wife may feel like the husband is lying to her. But if she is aware of what is available she will help to make ends meet.

Plan together

Husband and wife need to both agree on their financial plans and goals. Pray together about your finances. Plan what you want to do with "God's" money. Plan how you want to give. Plan how you want to invest. Plan how you want to save. Plan your family development projects. Do this with much prayer and discussion.

Because you have different minds it will take a lot of effort to come together on financial issues. Both partners may have different goals and different priorities when it comes to financial issues. Men generally tend to focus on the long-term plans, while women see the daily needs at home. This can result in disagreements in financial decisions. Instead, recognize that both perspectives are needed and some compromise is necessary.

Also recognize that God has given the man in the home the major responsibility for earning. The husband feels this burden much differently than the wife. He takes pride in providing and is devastated when he is unable to do so or when there is lack in the home. When he loses a job it hits deeply at his sense of worth. He desperately needs an encouraging partner at such a time. A small comment by the wife about financial needs can be taken by the husband as an attack on his manhood and he can respond defensively. Because of these feelings it takes lots of love and understanding to be open and to plan together.

Verbally agree that you won't make major decisions without agreeing together. An idea that has helped many couples is to set a limit on the amount that each can spend without consulting the other. You may feel that this is limiting but remember that you are partners. When you make an unwise decision in your family it will affect both of you. A good decision will benefit both of you.

Decide together who will be responsible for different financial transactions. Who will pay the house rent? Who buys the clothes for the children? Who does the banking?

Don't just assume that the husband always does some things. Maybe in your father's home it was that way, but there may be a better solution in your home. In some cases the wife is much better at keeping records or in budgeting the money. In such a case, a wise husband will gladly allow her to bless the family with that strength.

If one spouse has the spiritual gift of giving, the couple should talk about how to use that for the glory of God without adversely affecting the family. It is probably not wise to have the "giver" control the finances. When the giver meets someone with a need on the way home, the money intended for meat suddenly "meets" another need!

Many Christians have a hard time planning. They prefer to "walk by faith" or be "led by the Spirit." However, the Bible clearly supports planning. Consider these verses:

Luke 14:28, *"Suppose one of you wants to build a tower. Will he not first sit down and estimate the cost to see if he has enough money to complete it?"*

Prov. 16:3,9 *"Commit to the LORD whatever you do, and your plans will succeed. In his heart a man plans his course, but the LORD determines his steps."*

Often finances are a problem because of lack of planning. All of us deal with money in our lives and in our homes but many of us fail to plan. And as is the case in all areas of life, **"TO FAIL TO PLAN IS TO PLAN TO FAIL."** What is involved in making financial plans?

1. Planning involves evaluating

Planning involves taking an honest look at all your finances, your income, debts, investments, etc. Decide what changes you need to make and then begin to live by your plan. If you don't stop to evaluate, you will not be able to plan properly.

2. Planning involves recording

If you cannot tell me how you spent your money last month I can tell you that you don't have a very good plan. How much did you spend on transportation? How much for food? Recording expenses is the first step towards preparing a budget that you can live by. Get a notebook and start keeping a record of where your money is going. It will help you a great deal in planning. It takes time and effort to keep records but it will pay off in the long run. You will never again moan 5 days before you get paid, "What ever happened to my money?"

3. Planning involves budgeting

Budgeting is simply putting down on paper what you expect to earn and what you expect to spend. I am not suggesting that we can control every aspect of our financial lives. We live in a changing world and many things are out of our control. But we are called to plan and to live wisely. This is so crucial for family finances that we need to look at it more closely.

Budget together

It is difficult to reach financial goals without a budget. A budget is simply a plan of how you will use the resources that you anticipate receiving. It should include all expected sources of income as well as all planned expenses. Include plans for tithing, giving, and saving as well as rent, food, etc.

A budget is beneficial in several areas. It helps you to **evaluate priorities** and to determine in advance what you want to do. A budget helps you to **meet your financial** goals. For example, in your budget you can plan for monthly savings that will help to purchase the land you desire. It also helps greatly to **control expenses.** When you work with a budget you will always have one eye on the amount allowed for that item. This greatly helps to **resist impulsive spending**. A budget also greatly **helps reduce tension** between spouses. It might be difficult to agree on the budget but once you have set the budget you don't need to argue about many things. All you need to ask is, "Is it in the budget?"

A good budget will include plans for giving, saving, and one time expenses such as clothes or school fees. You should even think of budgeting for "emergencies" such as sicknesses. Sometimes we create "emergencies" by failing to plan. I remember several times being awakened in the middle of the night with someone knocking desperately at the door. They needed transportation to the hospital because their wife was "sick." They didn't have money for transportation because it was an "emergency." I would pull myself out of bed and go for the patient only to find a pregnant wife in the midst of labour! I felt like saying, "Brother, you've had nine months to prepare for this event, don't call it an emergency!" (Don't worry, I never actually said it!) Don't wait until your wife is ready to deliver to think about the cost of having a baby! Let's look at some suggestions for making a budget.

A budget should be specific

A good budget must be as specific as possible. It should include actual amounts, not vague ideas. Use the records you have been keeping to make sure that you have a category for every type of expense that you have.

A budget should be realistic

A budget won't work if it is not realistic. The income and expenses should balance each other. If they don't balance on paper you can be sure that they won't in real life!

Can you really eat with the amount budgeted for food? If not, an adjustment needs to be made. Remember to plan for some emergencies. Sometimes there will be unexpected travel or sickness that requires money. Is it in your budget?

Make sure that your income amounts are also realistic. Don't budget for money that you're not sure of receiving. If you are in business or sales you will need to plan carefully since monthly income can fluctuate greatly. Make sure you don't spend everything when you have a good month! Your budget should help you through the difficult times.

A budget should be adjusted

Every budget may need to be adjusted to fit realities. Income sometimes goes up or down depending on job situations, the economy or even the weather. Costs may also fluctuate and adjustments will need to be made. It is good to evaluate at the end of the month how well you were able to stick to the budget of the previous month and make any necessary changes. After a couple of months you can get a clear idea of whether or not your budget needs some adjustments. You may find that in some areas you have put more than enough and in another area it was very difficult. You can then agree together to adjust the budget accordingly.

See *Appendix C* for sample budgets and more practical tips for a budget.

4. Planning involves long as well as short-term goals.

In your planning you should first look at the short-term goals that you have for yourself or your family. This may include getting out of debt or starting to save. But you should also look at the long-term issues such as purchasing land, saving for retirement, etc.

In a recent testimony service at our church, a sister stood up to share that God had enabled her and her husband to build a house. She specifically mentioned that one thing which had really helped them was to write down a specific financial goal of savings for each month. Once they committed themselves to that goal, their dream became a reality.

Planning together takes time and effort. But the unity that comes when you agree together is worth the effort. Set a time now when you will sit and plan together. Make sure it is a time that you are both relaxed and able to concentrate. Talk together through the issues that have been raised in this book. You may find that you need to seek out the advice of a financial consultant who can give a good perspective on reaching your long term goals.

FINANCES SHOULD BE TAUGHT TO CHILDREN

A third principle of finances in the home is that financial principles should be taught to children. You are responsible to teach your children all things, including how to handle money. The Bible says in Prov. 22:6, *"Train a child in the way he should go, and when he is old he will not turn from it."* And in Eph. 6:4, it adds, *"...bring them up in the training and instruction of the Lord."* In most families the area of financial training is woefully neglected. Most children leave home and enter the world with very little idea of how to properly handle money. We should have a goal that when our child reaches adulthood he/she will know how to handle money in a mature way.

We need to teach children first of all by our example. We cannot teach them God's principles until we ourselves are living in obedience to the word of God. But after living a good example we need to deliberately teach them some things. What do we teach them about money?

Teach them the value of work

Let them work. Let them realize that work produces money. Money does not mysteriously appear from Daddy's pocket; it comes from work! You can explain how you work and how you are paid and then what happens to the money. As your children grow, teach them to associate work with money.

Assign them some tasks that you will give them money for rather than just giving them money when they ask for it. When they want to go to Jr. Youth camp give them a month to "earn" that money. Give them a small amount for cleaning their room, a similar amount for working outside in the garden or yard, etc. (Adjust the amount to fit the age of your child and what is being done.) You can encourage you children to read by "paying" them when they read a book and write you a report. You can do the same for scripture memory. Be creative. I am not saying that we need to pay our children to do the work that we expect them to do. But remember the goal that when your child leaves home and is on his own he/she will know how to manage money. You need to start training them early.

Many people raising children today grew up in homes where they were required to do a lot of physical work. I'm afraid that many of them thought to themselves, *When I have children, I'll make sure that they don't have to work as I did.* Their intention is good; however, I encourage you to think about what will happen when a generation of children grow up who don't know how to work. Their idea of work is pushing the remote control buttons as they watch TV! Work is not bad and children need to learn how to work. Don't overdo it, but do it! If you have someone helping you in your home, don't allow that person to do everything for your child. Give them some daily responsibilities in the home. Find jobs for them to do. Even at an early age they can learn to sweep, burn trash, brush shoes, wash the car, plant flowers, fold clothes and many other jobs around the house. I give my children a list of jobs every Saturday that I expect them to do. Every week I change some things around so that it doesn't become boring and sometimes throw in fun things like preparing a drama for the family that evening.   I want them to realize that they are a part of a team effort and that they can play a part in what needs to be done.

Teach them the value of money

As you learn and apply scriptural principles of finance in your life, pass this on to your children. Discuss financial issues with them. Share scriptures with them about money. Make observations from life. Share with them appropriate information about lessons you've learned about finances. This includes also teaching them the dangers of money.   Help them to learn contentment. Have them memorize the verse that says, "Godliness with contentment is great gain." Talk to them about what advertising does to our desire for things.

Involve them in praying for God's provision of finances for a certain need. This teaches them to learn to trust God for things and to wait on his provision. If you are praying for money for school fees, involve the children.

The best way for them to learn the value of money is by handling it physically. Let them work for some money. Then give them some discretion in how they use it. They may still buy sweets, but they'll think twice about spending all their hard earned money on something that disappears in 10 minutes.

Teach them the value of giving

Teach your children to give. Show them that you are giving and encourage them also to give. When people have needs, involve them in giving to meet the needs. Encourage giving in other ways.   Ask your child to give a toy to another child and praise him/her when they are willing to do it. Involve the family in giving to special projects, fund raisings, etc. Especially if they are older, ask for suggestions about how to make money to give, or what can be sacrificed for the sake of giving. Maybe everyone can agree to do without bread for breakfast one morning to have more to give away. Make it a family project.

Instill in your children the value of tithing. Do it as soon as they are given any money, no matter how little. I clearly remember what my parents did with money that they gave to me. Of every 10 cents I was to give 1 cent to the church. My wife's parents worked in a similar way and as a result of that childhood training we have never disagreed in our marriage about tithing.

Teach them the value of saving

At an early age you can teach your children the value of saving money which is such an important principle of handling finances. Our society teaches us to borrow; scripture encourages saving. If you are giving your child money or if he is earning it, insist that a certain amount goes into savings. Encourage him to save money to purchase a soccer ball or something else that he desires. Show by example that patience in finances is better than greed.

In order to teach these things to our children we started giving them ten coins each week when they were small. We trained them to give one to God, to save four and the remaining five they can spend as they want—with some parental guidance of course! If they want to buy a sweet, they can use their money. (This does wonders for child/parent confrontations in the supermarket. When your child asks, "May I get that sweet?", just reply, "If you have the money!") When I repair a puncture on my son's bicycle I "charge" him! Although the actual cost is more than he pays me he is learning that it costs something to repair a bicycle. That will help him not only to use money wisely but how to care for his own property well. If we just did everything for him, he would not learn these things as well. Giving an allowance teaches them how to save, how to give and how to be responsible. Their "savings" may be kept aside in a special place or a parent can simply keep a record of what is saved and be sure to have it available for the child when it is needed.

Of course, as parents we don't expect them to support themselves financially, but we are **deliberately teaching them how to handle money**. As they grow older we will increase the amount as well as the responsibility. By the time they are teenagers they should be able to earn money and do things like buying their own clothes. A parent should work with the teenager to develop a budget that will incorporate the principles taught in scripture. Make a plan of what you will "pay" your teenager to do and help him/her develop a budget. You might include household chores that they are responsible to do, reading books, memorizing scripture, daily Bible reading, etc. They will clearly see the connection between their effort and their income. Allow them to start paying for some of their expenses that you have been doing as a parent. Give them more and more responsibility for purchasing their own clothes, miscellaneous school supplies, etc. Allow them to make mistakes with small amounts of money and when they are adults, they will know how to manage more substantial amounts. Think about the application of these principles for your situation and your children. The power is not in any particular formulae, but in the deliberate effort you are making to train your children about life and money!

TEACH YOUR CHILDREN ABOUT MONEY. Start today.

God has a plan for your family, including finances. Determine to follow his plan, work together, teach your children and you will find that God's way is by far the best. It is not easy to put all these things into practice but you can do it! Start now and unlock God's blessing in your life.

Action Point: Reflect on how finances are handled in your home. What needs to change? What specific steps will you take as result of reading this chapter? Below are some suggestions to guide you. Put an "x" in front of the ones you will do.

_____ Talk to my spouse about our financial situation
_____ Begin keeping a record of how we spend money
_____ Prepare a budget
_____ Develop a long term savings and investment plan
_____ Write a will
_____ Get life insurance
_____ See a financial advisor to get financial advice
_____ Have a Bible study with our children to discuss financial
　　　　principles
_____ Begin giving an allowance to our children
_____ Develop a plan for our children to "work" for some money
_____ Other:

Conclusion

We have examined a lot of material on finances, each of them crucial aspects of God's plan for our lives. I hope you recognize that financial freedom is more than just obeying God's will in one area of our lives. It involves a continual effort to apply biblical principles in all areas. This book is only an introduction to what God has to say about our money; use it as a springboard to dig deeper and to learn more.

I believe with all my heart that God wants you to experience financial freedom and I fully believe that the principles contained in this book will lead you on an exciting journey towards that freedom. My prayer is that God will give you joy as you take steps of obedience in that journey and that your life will be an example to many others. Remember that change takes time and don't grow discouraged if you don't see immediate changes. Keep sowing the right seeds and you will be assured of reaping the right harvest!

If you are a pastor or church leader, I encourage you to first of all put this book into practice in your life. Then use it as a tool for teaching those whom you are leading. Use the *Bible Study Guide* which follows if you have small groups that can discuss these principles. What a joy it will be to see the transformation in your group!

"So if the Son sets you free, you will be free indeed." (Jn. 8:36)

Appendix A:
Verses from Proverbs dealing with finances, wealth and work

Prov 1:19 Such is the end of all who go after ill-gotten gain; it takes away the lives of those who get it.

Prov 3:2 For they will prolong your life many years and bring you prosperity.

Prov 3:9 Honor the LORD with your wealth, with the first fruits of all your crops;

Prov 3:10 Then your barns will be filled to overflowing, and your vats will brim over with new wine.

Prov 3:13-16 Blessed is the man who finds wisdom, the man who gains understanding, for she is more profitable than silver and yields better returns than gold. She is more precious than rubies; nothing you desire can compare with her. Long life is in her right hand; in her left hand are riches and honor.

Prov 5:10 Lest strangers feast on your wealth and your toil enrich another man's house.

Prov 6:1-5 My son, if you have put up security for your neighbor, if you have struck hands in pledge for another, if you have been trapped by what you said, ensnared by the words of your mouth, then do this, my son, to free yourself, since you have fallen into your neighbor's hands: Go and humble yourself; press your plea with your neighbor! Allow no sleep to your eyes, no slumber to your eyelids. Free yourself, like a gazelle from the hand of the hunter, like a bird from the snare of the fowler.

Prov 6:10-11 A little sleep, a little slumber, a little folding of the hands to rest— and poverty will come on you like a bandit and scarcity like an armed man.

Prov 6:31 Yet if he is caught, he must pay sevenfold, though it costs him all the wealth of his house.

Prov 7:20 He took his purse filled with money and will not be home till full moon.

Prov 8:10-11 Choose my instruction instead of silver, knowledge rather than choice gold, for wisdom is more precious than rubies, and nothing you desire can compare with her.

Prov 8:18-19 With me are riches and honor, enduring wealth and prosperity. My fruit is better than fine gold; what I yield surpasses choice silver.

Prov 8:21 Bestowing wealth on those who love me and making their treasuries full.

Prov 10:2 Ill-gotten treasures are of no value, but righteousness delivers from death.

Prov 10:4 Lazy hands make a man poor, but diligent hands bring wealth.

Prov 10:15-16 The wealth of the rich is their fortified city, but poverty is the ruin of the poor. The wages of the righteous bring them life, but the income of the wicked brings them punishment.

Prov 10:22 The blessing of the LORD brings wealth, and he adds no trouble to it.

Prov 11:4 Wealth is worthless in the day of wrath, but righteousness delivers from death.

Prov 11:15-16 He who puts up security for another will surely suffer, but whoever refuses to strike hands in pledge is safe. A kindhearted woman gains respect, but ruthless men gain only wealth.

Prov 11:18 The wicked man earns deceptive wages, but he who sows righteousness reaps a sure reward.

Prov 11:24-25 One man gives freely, yet gains even more; another withholds unduly, but comes to poverty. A generous man will prosper; he who refreshes others will himself be refreshed.

Prov 11:28-29 Whoever trusts in his riches will fall, but the righteous will thrive like a green leaf. He who brings trouble on his family will inherit only wind, and the fool will be servant to the wise.

Prov 12:11 He who works his land will have abundant food, but he who chases fantasies lacks judgment.

Prov 12:27 The lazy man does not roast his game, but the diligent man prizes his possessions.

Prov 13:4 The sluggard craves and gets nothing, but the desires of the diligent are fully satisfied.

Prov 13:7-8 One man pretends to be rich, yet has nothing; another pretends to be poor, yet has great wealth. A man's riches may ransom his life, but a poor man hears no threat.

Prov 13:11 Dishonest money dwindles away, but he who gathers money little by little makes it grow.

Prov 13:22 A good man leaves an inheritance for his children's children, but a sinner's wealth is stored up for the righteous.

Prov 14:4 Where there are no oxen, the manger is empty, but from the strength of an ox comes an abundant harvest.

Prov 14:20 The poor are shunned even by their neighbors, but the rich have many friends.

Prov 14:23-24 All hard work brings a profit, but mere talk leads only to poverty. The wealth of the wise is their crown, but the folly of fools yields folly.

Prov 14:31 He who oppresses the poor shows contempt for their Maker, but whoever is kind to the needy honors God.

Prov 15:6 The house of the righteous contains great treasure, but the income of the wicked brings them trouble.

Prov 15:16-17 Better a little with the fear of the LORD than great wealth with turmoil. Better a meal of vegetables where there is love than a fattened calf with hatred.

Prov 15:27 A greedy man brings trouble to his family, but he who hates bribes will live.

Prov 16:8 Better a little with righteousness than much gain with injustice.

Prov 16:16 How much better to get wisdom than gold, to choose understanding rather than silver!

Prov 16:19-20 Better to be lowly in spirit and among the oppressed than to share plunder with the proud. Whoever gives heed to instruction prospers, and blessed is he who trusts in the LORD.

Prov 16:26 The laborer's appetite works for him; his hunger drives him on.

Prov 17:1-2 Better a dry crust with peace and quiet than a house full of feasting, with strife. A wise servant will rule over a disgraceful son, and will share the inheritance as one of the brothers.

Prov 17:5 He who mocks the poor shows contempt for their Maker; whoever gloats over disaster will not go unpunished.

Prov 17:16 Of what use is money in the hand of a fool, since he has no desire to get wisdom?

Prov 17:18 A man lacking in judgment strikes hands in pledge and puts up security for his neighbor.

Prov 18:9 One who is slack in his work is brother to one who destroys.

Prov 18:11 The wealth of the rich is their fortified city; they imagine it an unscalable wall.

Prov 18:23 A poor man pleads for mercy, but a rich man answers harshly.

Prov 19:1 Better a poor man whose walk is blameless than a fool whose lips are perverse.

Prov 19:4 Wealth brings many friends, but a poor man's friend deserts him.

Prov 19:6 -7 Many curry favor with a ruler, and everyone is the friend of a man who gives gifts. A poor man is shunned by all his relatives—how much more do his friends avoid him! Though he pursues them with pleading, they are nowhere to be found.

Prov 19:10 It is not fitting for a fool to live in luxury—how much worse for a slave to rule over princes!

Prov 19:14-15 Houses and wealth are inherited from parents, but a prudent wife is from the LORD. Laziness brings on deep sleep, and the shiftless man goes hungry.

Prov 19:17 He who is kind to the poor lends to the LORD, and he will reward him for what he has done.

Prov 19:22 What a man desires is unfailing love; better to be poor than a liar.

Prov 20:15-17 Gold there is, and rubies in abundance, but lips that speak knowledge are a rare jewel. Take the garment of one who puts up security for a stranger; hold it in pledge if he does it for a wayward woman. Food gained by fraud tastes sweet to a man, but he ends up with a mouth full of gravel.

Prov 20:21 An inheritance quickly gained at the beginning will not be blessed at the end.

Prov 21:5-6 The plans of the diligent lead to profit as surely as haste leads to poverty. A fortune made by a lying tongue is a fleeting vapor and a deadly snare.

Prov 21:14 A gift given in secret soothes anger, and a bribe concealed in the cloak pacifies great wrath.

Prov 21:17 He who loves pleasure will become poor; whoever loves wine and oil will never be rich.

Prov 21:20-21 In the house of the wise are stores of choice food and oil, but a foolish man devours all he has. He who pursues righteousness and love finds life, prosperity and honor.

Prov 21:26 All day long he craves for more, but the righteous give without sparing.

Prov 22:1-2 A good name is more desirable than great riches; to be esteemed is better than silver or gold. Rich and poor have this in common: The LORD is the Maker of them all.

Prov 22:4 Humility and the fear of the LORD bring wealth and honor and life.

Prov 22:7 The rich rule over the poor, and the borrower is servant to the lender.

Prov 22:9 A generous man will himself be blessed, for he shares his food with the poor.

Prov 22:16 He who oppresses the poor to increase his wealth and he who gives gifts to the rich—both come to poverty.

Prov 22:22 Do not exploit the poor because they are poor and do not crush the needy in court.

Prov 22:26-27 Do not be a man who strikes hands in pledge or puts up security for debts; if you lack the means to pay, your very bed will be snatched from under you.

Prov 23:4-7 Do not wear yourself out to get rich; have the wisdom to show restraint. Cast but a glance at riches, and they are gone, for they will surely sprout wings and fly off to the sky like an eagle. Do not eat the food of a stingy man, do not crave his delicacies; for he is the kind of man who is always thinking about the cost. "Eat and drink," he says to you, but his heart is not with you.

Prov 23:8 You will vomit up the little you have eaten and will have wasted your compliments.

Prov 23:20-21 Do not join those who drink too much wine or gorge themselves on meat, for drunkards and gluttons become poor, and drowsiness clothes them in rags.

Prov 24:33-34 A little sleep, a little slumber, a little folding of the hands to rest—and poverty will come on you like a bandit and scarcity like an armed man.

Prov 27:13 Take the garment of one who puts up security for a stranger; hold it in pledge if he does it for a wayward woman.

Prov 27:23-24 Be sure you know the condition of your flocks, give careful attention to your herds; for riches do not endure forever, and a crown is not secure for all generations.

Prov 27:25-27 When the hay is removed and new growth appears and the grass from the hills is gathered in, the lambs will provide you with clothing, and the goats with the price of a field. You will have plenty of goats' milk to feed you and your family and to nourish your servant girls.

Prov 28:3 A ruler who oppresses the poor is like a driving rain that leaves no crops.

Prov 28:6 Better a poor man whose walk is blameless than a rich man whose ways are perverse.

Prov 28:8 He who increases his wealth by exorbitant interest amasses it for another, who will be kind to the poor.

Prov 28:10-11 He who leads the upright along an evil path will fall into his own trap, but the blameless will receive a good inheritance. A rich man may be wise in his own eyes, but a poor man who has discernment sees through him.

Prov 28:19-20 He who works his land will have abundant food, but the one who chases fantasies will have his fill of poverty. A faithful man will be richly blessed, but one eager to get rich will not go unpunished.

Prov 28:22 A stingy man is eager to get rich and is unaware that poverty awaits him.

Prov 28:25 A greedy man stirs up dissension, but he who trusts in the LORD will prosper.

Prov 28:27 He who gives to the poor will lack nothing, but he who closes his eyes to them receives many curses.

Prov 29:3 A man who loves wisdom brings joy to his father, but a companion of prostitutes squanders his wealth.

Prov 29:7 The righteous care about justice for the poor, but the wicked have no such concern.

Prov 30:8-9 Keep falsehood and lies far from me; give me neither poverty nor riches, but give me only my daily bread. Otherwise, I may have too much and disown you and say, 'Who is the LORD?' Or I may become poor and steal, and so dishonor the name of my God.

Prov 31:16 She considers a field and buys it; out of her earnings she plants a vineyard.

Prov 31:18 She sees that her trading is profitable, and her lamp does not go out at night.

Prov 31:20 -21 She opens her arms to the poor and extends her hands to the needy. When it snows, she has no fear for her household; for all of them are clothed in scarlet.

Prov 31:24 She makes linen garments and sells them, and supplies the merchants with sashes.

Appendix B:
Questions about tithing.

1. What can I do about tithing when my husband is not a believer?

This is a difficult issue for many wives and my heart goes out to you if you are in this situation. My advice is for you to explain to your husband what you believe about God's promise of blessing and request to give a certain portion for one year (or another specific time period) and see if your finances are better off or not. Propose that if you're worse off, stop giving; if you're better off continue or increase! If your husband agrees, then take God at his word and see what will happen. If your husband refuses, accept his decision as the leader in the home and continue praying. Don't feel guilty about the issue of money, nor try to give secretly. If you have income over which your husband has given you complete control you can tithe on that income but you should respect your husband's wishes. God will not hold you responsible for his decision since he is the head of the home.

2. Is it right to tithe to a ministry or other organization?

God's word says that we are to bring the tithe into the storehouse. We normally take this to be the local church. It is the will of God for every believer to be involved and committed to a local church, under the authority of a pastor. To this church the believer should give his/her tithe. As God directs you may also decide to support other worthy ministries and groups, but this is in addition to your tithe. The local church needs you and you need the local church. It will be hard for your heart to be fully committed to the church if you are not giving there. The local church can also consider supporting ministries from their budget. If all members would be faithful this would be possible.

3. I have a church at "home" where I send my tithe; here where I work they don't need it as much. What can you comment?

In many cultures this creates a dilemma for people who want to be faithful. It is not an easy issue. Decide where your loyalty is. Look at where you are being fed spiritually. I don't believe it is right to go to a local church to eat spiritually and then you send all your tithes back to a church that you visit only occasionally. Perhaps you can tithe to the church you attend regularly and send an offering or gift to the church at home. Part of the issue is commitment. Be committed where you are at the moment. Put your heart and soul there and serve the Lord in that place with your time, prayers, and finances. If God calls you to another place, trust him to find another church where you can again commit yourself. If the church where you have roots is more needy, is it possible to work at a partner relationship with your current church in a way that both would benefit?

4. Do I pay from the "gross" or the "take home" pay?

I dealt with this briefly in the section on tithing and said that I believe we should tithe from the gross. Here's why I believe that. The gross pay reflects the amount that we have truly earned. Any deductions are payments or expenditures that are made on my behalf by my employer before he gives me the balance. This is true even of taxes that are not voluntary! That is an expense that I owe to the government. Other dues and deductions are also payments. Think of it this way. What if your salary was 10,000 but your employer paid for your rent, put money automatically into a savings scheme, paid for transport, paid for medical insurance and then only gave you a small balance of 1000 for food and miscelaneous items. What is your true income? You can't say 1000, although that is all that you received in your hand at the end of the month.

At the same time, I don't believe that God is legalistic. He knows our hearts and our desires. If you are not tithing at all, take a step and start tithing on the take home pay. But have the goal to give fully and even beyond the tithe. Some persons have so badly handled their money that they hardly have any take home pay at all after deductions and loan repayments are dealt with. Such persons should begin being faithful as they are able and continue to increase their giving.

Appendix C:
Sample Budgets

The following budgets are given as a sample for three different levels of income. Your family's income and expenses will be different but this will help you to see what a budget looks like. If the figures aren't realistic in your currency, use the ratios as a rough guide.

INCOME:	Family 1	Family 2	Family 3
Husband	5,000	10,000	20,000
Wife	3,000	8,000	15,000
Total income	8,000	18,000	35,000
EXPENSES:			
Tithe	800	1,800	3,500
Offerings/Giving	200	1000	1800
Housing (rent, supplies)	1,000	5,000	10,000
Food	2,000	3,500	5,000
Clothes	200	800	1200
Transportation	400	800	4000(car)
School Fees	900	1000	3000
Extended Family	200	500	1500
Savings	800	1000	2000
House Help	700	900	1500
Medical	300	800	2000
Misc.	500	1200	3500
Total expenses	8000	16,500	35,000

Some suggestions for a budget:

1. Set aside the money for different things in different envelopes. For example, if the wife is responsible for the food, give her the amount for food. She can purchase major items at one time and actually save some money for the family in that way. She will know at all times what is remaining for food. Label each envelope with the category, "Transport", "Food", etc. Take care that you don't yield to the temptation to "borrow" from one category to increase the resources of another unless you have both agreed to do so.

2. Note that some items will not always be used. For example medical expenses come occasionally. School fees are due at certain times. This money needs to be set aside or if possible banked so that it will be there when needed.

3. It is important to know at the end of the month if you have reached your goal. This can be done by checking the envelopes if you have used that system, or by writing down how the money is spent each time you spend. This becomes very important if you have not used envelopes. A notebook can be used to write down each expenditure. The totals at the end of the month will show how much you have spent in each category. When you see how you have done you will know where you need to improve or in which area you need to change your budget to make it more realistic.

Appendix D:
Bible Study Guide

This Bible Study guide can be used as an independent study or together with teaching done in the church. However, it assumes that the members of the group are familiar with what has been covered in the booklet. Our study is to take us deeper into the topic and allow the members to discover for themselves what the Bible teaches on this important subject. If the keys are taught in the church on a weekly basis and the Bible Study Guide is used in small groups, the impact will be the greatest.

If the 7 Keys are taught in the church, use the following schedule to mesh with the Bible study Guide.

Week One: Keys One and Two, Recognize Finances as a Spiritual Issue, Learn Contentment

Week Two: Key Three, Obey Biblical Principles of Earning

Week Three: Key Four, Avoid Debt

Week Four: Key Five, Learn to Tithe

Week Five: Key Six, Learn to Give

Week Six: Key Seven, Manage Finances in the Home

Tips for Bible Study leader:
➢ Questions are in bold print.
➢ Involve all members. You may need to direct a question to someone who has been quiet or ask, "Can someone who hasn't contributed so far answer this question?"
➢ Prepare by reading the scripture and reading through the questions on your own time.
➢ If group members each purchase the book *7 Keys to Financial Freedom* it will be helpful to you.
➢ Note that these discussion questions are based on the NIV version. If you are using a different version make sure to read the verses in your translation before the meeting.
➢ Show enthusiasm! This study will change your group!
➢ Allow God to teach you as you teach others.

Week One
Keys: Recognize Finances as a Spiritual Issue & Learn Contentment

Introduction:

We are beginning our study of what the Bible teaches about finances. It will open our eyes to areas that we have not thought about before. Let's be open as we search the word of God and allow God to change each one of us. The more that we walk in obedience in our finances the more that we will experience God's blessings. We will be looking at "7 Keys of Financial Freedom." In this session we will study the first two.

1. Review: What is Key One?

2. Read Mt. 6:24. What do you think it means when it says, "You cannot serve both God and money"?

3. Read Mt. 13:22. Comment, "Here Jesus talks about the 'deceitfulness of wealth'". In what ways can riches be deceitful?

4. We learned that God can use finances to direct our lives either by providing or withholding. Can you share an experience in which God guided you by *providing*? Can you share an experience in which he guided you by *withholding* finances?

5. Why do you think God sometimes withholds finances from us? What should we do when we lack finances?

6. Read Lk. 16:10-11. What do these verses teach about finances?

7. Do you agree or disagree with this statement, and why? "The way we handle our money says more about the condition of our heart than our testimony." For personal reflection, "Then what heart condition would your money show?"

8. Review: What was Key Two?
   Read Prov. 11:28. What does it mean to "trust in riches"?

9. Read Phil. 4:11-12. What had Paul learned and how do you think he learned it?

10. Read Heb. 13:5. What does this verse teach us about contentment?

11. Read 1 Tim. 6:9-10. What happens to people who want to get rich?
    What temptations do people face when they want to get rich?
    Does this mean it is a sin to be rich? Explain your answer.

12. Read Prov. 22:1. What does this verse teach us about character and money?
    If we believed this verse, what would it change in our lives?

13. Read Haggai 2:8, Ps. 50:10 and Lev. 25:23. What do these verses mean for us?
    If God owns everything, what am I supposed to do with the things that I have?
    What difference will this concept make in your life?

14. The deed of transfer. Remind the members of the deed of transfer that they signed during the teaching. If some were not present show it to them. Ask, What happened to you as you signed this deed of transfer? Has it changed your thinking in any way?

Conclusion

Conclude with prayer, especially praying that money and possessions will be properly understood by each one and that each one will be able to release his or her possessions to God and learn contentment.

Week Two
Key: Obey Biblical Principals of Earning

Introduction: How do we get money? Is there a right or wrong way to earn our daily bread? What does God say about how we obtain our money? That's what we want to look at in this study.

1. How many of the 7 principles for earning money can you remember?

2. Read Eph. 6:5-8. (Note: Instead of slaves and masters we use this scripture to teach about workers and bosses.) What does this passage teach us about our work?
    What would happen if all of us would obey these verses at our jobs?

3. Read Prov. 6:10-11. What does this verse teach about resting?
    Read 2 Thes. 3:6-12. (KJV says, "walketh disorderly" instead of "idle".) What do these verses teach us about people who pray for work but aren't ready to work hard?

    How do we do this?

4. Read Prov. 23:4. In what ways can we "wear ourselves out" to get rich?
    Why will God not bless working too much?

5. Read Prov. 22:16. In which ways have you seen the poor oppressed in the last month?
    Are we guilty of these things in any way?

6. Read Prov. 21:6. Is it possible to get rich by lying?
    What common ways of lying to earn money are used in our society today?
    Which ones are most common in your occupation?

7. Read Jer. 17:22. Why do you think God commanded that we shouldn't work on Sunday?
    What would you do in a case where an employer forces someone to work on Sunday?

8. Read Prov. 12:11. What are some "fantasies" that people chase today?

9. Do you believe this statement is biblical and what will be the result if we practice it? "Earn all you can, save all you can, and give all you can."

Conclusion
Pray for God to help each one to earn money in a way that is pleasing to God.
Pray for the unemployed in your group.
Pray for the businesses of the group members, for God's blessing to be upon them and for the owners to follow God's principles of earning.
Pray for those who may work on Sunday against their will.
Pray for each one to earn all he can, save all he can and give all he can.

Week Three
Key: Avoid Debt

Note. This key is probably the most difficult key for many people because it is so different from the way most have been taught and have experienced. Take enough time for honest discussion and to see what the Bible says about debt.

Introduction: All of us at one time or another have owed someone money. It is so common in our society that we don't even consider whether it is good or bad; we just accept that it is a part of life. But as we look at this lesson we will see what God says about debt and learn how we can be set free from debt.

1. Review. What were the five reasons given that debt is wrong?

2. Debt violates Scripture. Read Rom. 13:8 from several translations. What does this verse teach?
    What percentage of believers do you think live in disobedience to this verse?

3. Read Ps. 37:21. What is the contrast here between the righteous and the wicked?

4. Read Prov. 22:7. What does this verse say happens to the one who borrows money? How does a person become a slave when he/she has a debt?

According to this verse, what happens if you loan money to a friend?

After understanding this verse, what should we do when a friend wants to borrow from us?

5. Read Dt. 15:6 and 28:44. When God's people are in debt, what does it mean according to the second verse we read?

6. Read Phil. 4:19. This verse teaches that God will supply our needs. When we ask people to lend money to us, what does it say about our God?

7. Reflect on the verse you just read (Phil. 4:19). If it is true that "God will supply all our needs," what does it mean if he doesn't supply?

If you are praying for God to provide finances, how will you know when he answers positively?

If he doesn't want you to have the thing you are praying for at this time, how will he tell you?

Imagine that you are praying for something and God doesn't provide it in the time you want. So you go and get a loan and obtain the item. What has now happened to God's ability to speak to you?

8. Why is it so easy to get into debt?

9. Review. What are the steps to get out of debt?

Which of these steps is the most difficult for you? (See 2 Kings 4:7 for an example of selling things to repay a loan.)

Can anyone share how these steps have worked to set you free from debt?

10. What other questions do you have about debts?

Conclusion: Close with prayer, especially asking God…

• To set people free from the bondage of debts.

• For believers to clearly see God's teaching about debts

• Pray for courage for people to be willing to take the needed steps.

• For divine favour on those who are serious about getting out of debt.

Week Four:
Key Five: Learn to Tithe

Introduction: We have probably all heard sermons on tithing. Some of us have practiced it and have experienced God's blessing; others are still questioning many things about it. In this study we'll all come away with a better understanding of God's plan for us in this area.

1. Read Mal. 3:8-12. This passage is the basis for answering the questions which follow.   Make sure you get your answers to the following questions from this passage and not from your own head!

2. Why does Malachi say that the people are robbing God?
   How do you think God feels when his people "rob" him?

3. What is the result of failing to bring tithes and offerings to God?
   What happens when people are cursed and how does it apply to us?

4. What are all the blessings that God promises in these verses to those who obey?

5. Where are we supposed to tithe and why?
   Why do some people not want to bring their tithes to the church?

6. V. 10 says, "Bring the *WHOLE* tithe…" In what ways might we bring only a portion of our tithe?

7. What is the use of the tithe according to v. 10?
   What are the needs of the local church for which money is needed?

8. Read the following verses that deal with supporting the pastor. 1 Tim. 5:7-18; Gal. 6:6; 1 Cor. 9:14. What do these verses teach us?
   Does God expect pastors to "live by faith" financially? How well does our church obey these principles of pastoral support?

9. Can you give a testimony of God's faithfulness to his promises on tithing? (Allow individual responses depending on the time remaining.)

10. What other questions do you have about tithing?   (See Appendix B for answers to common questions.)

Conclusion:
   Pray for each member...

- To be faithful in tithing.

- To be faithful in giving offerings.

- To cheerfully support the pastors/church workers.

- To receive God's blessings on their lives as they walk in obedience.

Week Five
Key Six: Learn to Give

Introduction: In this session we will look at the sixth key, Learn to Give. Some of us are naturally more inclined to give; others are waiting to be given! Think about yourself as we begin. Would your best friend describe you as 'giver' or 'taker'? (Allow a moment for personal reflection.) This lesson will help all of us grow in the area of giving.

Read 2 Cor. 8:1-15 and then answer the following questions.

1. Why does God want us to be givers?
   Is it natural for us to give?
   What is the result of a spirit of dependency in our hearts?
   What does giving do to our hearts?

2. How does Paul describe the economic conditions facing the Macedonian churches in v. 2?
   Would you expect generous giving from such people?
   What can we learn from them?

3. Why were the Macedonian churches so eager to give?
   How can we become more like them?

4. When times are difficult, what can we do to give more?

5. What does verse 12 teach us about giving?

6. In v. 7 Paul challenges the Corinthian church to "excel" in the area of giving. How can we as a group/church learn to excel in this area?

7. Read 2 Cor. 9:6-11. What principles of giving can we learn from these verses?

Conclusion:

Identify a need that your group can give towards. It may be a need in the church; it may be a needy person/family in your area or any other need. Discuss how you can all give to meet that need and when you will do it. Remember to be creative and to give with joy, not compulsion.

Pray for God to stir the gift of giving in your group and to give each one a generous heart and willing attitude.

Week Six
Key Seven: Manage finances in the Home

Introduction: In this study we will look specifically at some principles related to handling finances in our homes. For those who are married we will discover some powerful principles. Also recognize that in your group there may be single mothers, widows or unmarried sisters or brothers. Include them in the discussion and allow them to share the unique challenges that face them. For the unmarried, this is a time that your thinking can be shaped for the time that you will have a home.

1ˢᵗ principle: Finances should be handled according to God's plan.

1. Think back to the home in which you grew up. How were finances handled? Who was in charge? Was there agreement? Was there any teaching of the children in this area?

Would you say that in the home where you grew up financial decisions were based on tradition and culture or the scriptures?

2nd principle: Finances should be handled together.

2. Read Gen. 2:24. What do you think becoming "one flesh" has to do with finances? What are some of the ways that this principle is violated in homes today?
    What is the result when finances are not dealt with openly in the home?

3. What keeps husbands and wives from planning their finances together?
    How can these be overcome?

4. What is the value of a budget?
    Can someone share from personal experience how he or she goes about the process of budgeting?

5. Read Prov. 16:3 and 16:9. Why does the Lord bless planning?

6. Prov. 21:20. Why is it so difficult to save?

3rd Principle: Finances should be taught to children.

7. Read Prov. 22:6 and Eph. 6:4. Does our training of children also include finances and what will be the result if we do?

8. How can we teach our children the value of work?

9. How can we teach our children the value of money?

10. How can we teach our children the value of giving?

11. How can we teach our children the value of saving?

Pray for finances in the homes and families of each person represented in your group. Pray especially for unity among couples in this area and for the couples in your group to be powerful examples of financial freedom.

As you conclude this study allow each person to share the most significant thing that they have learned about finances and what step they have taken or are taking in that area. Pray for each other in the areas mentioned. Encourage each one to continue reading and growing in the area of finances.

Bibliography

Avanzini, John. *Rapid Debt Reduction Strategies.* Hurst, TX: HIS Publishing Company, 1990.

Burkett, Larry. *What the Bible Says About Money* . Brentwood, TN.: Wolgemuth & Hyatt Publishers, Inc., 1989.

Dayton, Howard L., Jr. *Your Money: Frustration or Freedom?.* Wheaton,IL.: Tyndale House Publishers, 1983.

Dayton, Howard L., Jr. *Getting Out of Debt*, Wheaton,IL.: Tyndale House Publishers, 1986.

Gothard, Bill. *Institute in Basic Youth Conflicts, Research in Principles of Life.* USA: Institute in Basis Youth Conflicts, 1981.

Foster, Richard., *The Challenge of the Disciplined Life,* San Francisco, CA.:Harper and Row Publishers, 1985.

About the author

Rev. Jon Byler is currently working with Global Disciples as the international coordinator of the Global LEAD Alliance. He served for 13 years in Kenya where he was the director of the Centre for Christian Discipleship, a ministry devoted to equipping Kenyan leaders with tools needed for effective service. He established Leadership Training Institute and served as a pastor in two churches. He is happily married to Loice and God has blessed them with three children.

He is the author of several booklets:
The Heart of Christian Leadership
The Art of Christian Leadership
Preaching to Change Lives, a homiletics textbook
Use that Gift, a study of spiritual gifts
Pits, Prisons and Palaces, a study of the life of Joseph
Steps to Maturity, a 10-lesson discipleship course
Free at Last, a study of deliverance
The Christian and Authority
The Church With a Purpose, Bible Study Series

Contact him through:
Jon@LeadersServe.com

Notes: